CU01020047

THE ARCADIA GUIDE TO
BIO-ACTIVITY AND THE THEORY OF WILD RE-CREATION™
JOHN COURTENEY-SMITH MRSB

Bio-Activity and the Theory of Wild Re-Creation™
Copyright © John Courteney-Smith MRSB
Published: May 2016
ISBN: 978-0-0576570-3-8
Publisher: Arcadia Products PLC

For more information and our other reptile-keeping titles
please visit www.arcadia-uk.com

Contents

Foreword by
David Alderton

An exciting revolution is currently taking place in the keeping of reptiles and amphibians. This is the direct result of a combination of significant advances in our understanding of their care needs, matched by dramatic improvements in technology over recent years. The idea of having a vivarium full of thriving, living plants was simply not feasible until very recently - but it is now easily achievable, as explained in the following pages.

What have been the difficulties in the past? Well, firstly, the necessary lighting to allow plants to grow in these surroundings was not available. They soon failed to flourish and simply died back. The choice of substrates was very limited as well, and did not match the wild situation, where the soil is populated by a varied range of invertebrates. These creatures naturally play a vital role in helping to maintain the substrate in an optimal condition, so as to support plant growth and also recycle nutrients, as well as serving to supplement the diets of the resident reptiles or amphibians.

Now in this ground-breaking new title from John Courteney-Smith, one of the leading pioneers in this field, you can discover how at last, it is possible to set up a successful living vivarium of this type, which will become a thriving biological community. All of the information that you need, to achieve what has now become known in the hobby as Wild Re-creation™, is set out clearly on the following pages of this inspirational book.

As anyone who knows him will confirm, John is a very dedicated enthusiast, but more than that, he is in the fortunate position, as Reptile Products Manager for Arcadia, to make a real difference to the hobby. He has not only helped to pioneer the techniques, but also the equipment as well, from the lighting to the substrates and the supplements necessary to achieve this goal.

If you're fortunate enough to visit Arcadia's Head Office, you'll see an array of beautifully planted vivariums, housing a striking array of different reptiles and amphibians. Successful repeated breedings of what have previously been regarded as 'difficult' species such as pygmy chameleons have become commonplace in these surroundings.

Vivariums of this type undoubtedly look good, serving as a microcosm of the natural world. There is much that can be learnt from them, particularly as far as younger members of the family are concerned, bringing rather obscure concepts taught in the classroom, such as photosynthesis and ecosystems, to life.

Perhaps just as significantly though, a great deal of enjoyment can be gained simply by watching the vivarium occupants behave as they would in the wild in such surroundings. If you are serious about your hobby, you need this book. It is an informative and highly practical guide to this new era of Wild Re-creation™, written by the authority on the subject.

David Alderton, MA (Cantab.),
Editor, *Practical Reptile Keeping* magazine.

Introduction

et's be honest here: we, as a community, still really do not know all that much about the entire group of animals that we rather crudely lump together and refer to as 'exotics'. Okay, so we know how they 'tick', we understand the majority of the processes surrounding their organ function, but it is the 'why' and the 'eco-system synergy' that has, up until now, largely alluded us. It is true that these highly adapted and sentient species all play vital roles in the eco-systems in which they live, and, of course, they all have a vitally important impact upon the wider world. Imagine a world overrun with insects or rodents—well, remove the predators and that is what we could expect. Yes, they really are that important. A balance is required and, in nature, when left without interference, balance is maintained.

As keepers, we should embrace and enjoy every single aspect surrounding the care of our charges. We should take delight in watching their habits, territory maintenance and lifecycles, and we should marvel at their almost stealth-like appearance—but it doesn't stop there. More and more we are now starting to enjoy our animals as they start to truly thrive inside of the enclosures we provide for them. These enclosures/systems work in unison to provide for their own evolved needs and processes, per species, per enclosure. I mean, why sit and stare at a sterile, newspaper-laden plastic, wooden or glass box when you can enjoy a functioning and truly live micro-habitat—a slice of the desert or a piece of the jungle or a strip of the savannah right there in your own home? It is better for the animal in a whole host of ways and it will be vastly more fulfilling and enjoyable for the keeper. It really is a 'win win' situation.

Each and every species has its own defined space/territory and enriching tasks to fulfil each day to ensure that our world will continue to function in a homogenous way. As such, each species has changed and adapted over vast periods of time: they have learnt, as part of this process, how to not only survive but thrive in the predator-filled and vast expanse of the wild in which they are commonly/natively found. Of course, the core principle of evolution, by natural selection, is that every species will take all that it needs in the best way possible for itself, so that it is able to project its genes into as many generations to come as possible. In order to do this sustainably in the wild—that is, to replicate itself in a way where the species numbers are maintained and without biological detriment to the species itself—it simply has to constantly and consistently change and adapt, as does the earth around it. It has to take—that is, to use and assimilate—every single nutrient and mineral, even down to the macro level (each one is as important as the next in terms of full-spectrum and wild provision) that it needs and accordingly make use of the vast source of energy emanating from our sun that is all around it—doing so in a way that is the safest possible for that species.

So what does this mean for us as modern reptile keepers? Well, it means, of course, that we still have, and always will have, a vast amount left to learn. It means that our enclosures will be forever changing and adapting as new science and thinking emerges alongside new and ever-improving tech, and it also means that we should be able to start to breed some of the world's rarest species simply and efficiently, and therefore help to dramatically reduce the numbers of wild collected animals that are currently available.

'How do we do that?' I hear you ask? Well, it really is very simple. We look to the wild. We replicate the wild in captivity in a safe and measured way and allow nature to take its course. Just how we do that safely and effectively is the core consideration throughout this book.

For the purpose of this book, I will refer to Reptiles, Amphibians and Invertebrates as 'exotics' or simply as 'animals'. The core principles of care are the same for all species, and we can learn how to care for one species by reviewing the care for another. There are thousands of avenues to learning, each one as important as the last. As such, all of what I suggest in this book—every theological aspiration and thought, every bit of guidance and every single practice—can be applied to each and every other species in a way that is pertinent for it, whether it be Reptile, Amphibian, Invert or even Elephant, Human and everything in between. To mimic the evolved needs of a species is to provide for it accurately, whatever the species.

There also are some key points to be made. The chapters in this book are made up of some of the theories that I, and others like me, have developed over the years, in which I both passionately believe and which I use in my own systems daily. For me, this entire revelation has become an obsession of ongoing research and practise, one that is guided by a few simple processes and tasks, and has become encased in easy-to-understand terminology. As such, you will, in no doubt, see me refer to these processes almost continuously throughout this book. I will explain these processes and re-explain them in most chapters or make reference to them. I make no apology for this. It is vital in my mind that this theory is not only explained and debated at large, but that it is understood and that the good is taken from it and used to the benefit of animal welfare, which is where I must remain focused.

The watchword or banner here, of course, is the core and fundamental theory and the practice of safe and measured Wild Re-Creation™ through Bio-Activity. This is my theory and, for what it is worth, I sincerely hope that it helps you to propel your herpetological skills forward and to see a marked improvement in animal welfare and ethical reproduction in captivity.

John Courteney-Smith MRSB

"Agama Mwanzae Requires exact care, high heat, high UVB, a varied diet and lots of room"

Biodiversity is vital. It is all that is important and it is all that really matters with regard to the effective emulation and maintenance of a wild, thriving eco-system. These systems have developed over millennia to live and to work together in balance at all times, and to be able to constantly overcome those periods of hardship and of natural variation and/or disaster. We as humans must learn to respect and learn from this 'Biodiversity' and also 'acknowledge' the need for its long-term balance. Not only are the secrets of the earth itself hidden within these systems, like ancient relics just waiting to be discovered, but within lies a map, a map that will point exotic animal keepers and conservationists alike toward the pathway of effective Wild Re-Creation™ leading to ethical and effective captive care.

John Courteney-Smith, 2015

Wild Re-Creation™
through Bio-Activity

From this point onwards, you will see me use the phrase 'Wild Re-Creation™ through Bio-Activity'. This is the explanatory title given to describe my theory. Both of these terms are 'doing' words, but both have to be integrated into one another for the theory to work properly.

'Wild Re-Creation™' refers to a keeper of any given species seeking to replicate the core external parameters that interact with the species of which they seek to propagate when found in the wild. 'Bio-Activity' refers to a living culture that goes some way to sustain the ecosystem in a cyclical manner. In my mind, you cannot have one without the other.

In truth, Wild Re-Creation™, in terms of solar energy, is all well and good, and would be a great leap forward in captive care all on its own, but couple that together with the birth and ongoing maintenance of a 'live' culture, a micro habitat that helps to sustain and supply for a species, and you have the very first glimpses into the keys to both effective and ethical captive reptile care.

Wild Re-Creation™ is just that: the replication of the wild. Bio-Activity is a fizzing, living, breathing culture of 'earth, flora and fauna' that allow a keeper to delve deeper into the ever-changing world of effective care.

Wild re-creation, is it possible?

There are many assumptions banded about in the reptile-keeping hobby that I not only simply hate but that also can cause new keepers to fall foul of new and constantly evolving thought and process. One of these unhelpful and very untrue statements of course is that, 'These animals are not in the wild so how can they possibly have the same requirements as the wild animal?' or 'My pet is captive-bred from a long line of captive-produced animals... It's fine, I am sure. It's not wild, has never been and never will, so my care is fine.'

These assumptions are simply wrong and do not take biological diversity and function into mind. We cannot pretend that even twenty or thirty years of captive breeding can override X millions of years of wild change and adaption. Only the human animal is arrogant enough to suggest so. As is the case with many domesticated species, including our beloved dogs; even they still have the same biological needs and sometimes tendencies as the wild ancestor. By this I mean that the dog is still a livebearer

> *Wild Re-Creation™ is just that: the replication of the wild. Bio-Activity is a fizzing, living, breathing culture of 'earth, flora and fauna' that allow a keeper to delve deeper into the ever-changing world of effective care."*

that offers social care for young; they still have a need for water and, of course, food, and both still require the same types of food. And in fact, when dogs are 'free-roaming', they form packs and will scavenge and hunt in much the same way as the wild animal. This is just another indicator that further supports the notion that we cannot override the dictates of nature. Look at the recent C change in thinking behind the feeding of pet dogs, for example. We are now racing headlong into the realisation that dogs fair better on grain-free, with whole and raw meat sources, even with the inclusion of bone and fur at the extreme. This is vastly different to the advice given even two years ago when we were advised to use little meat or fish, and to provide lots of grain and plant matter. Of course, this directly points back to the adapted and biological requirement of the group, regardless of its pathway to domestication.

If we are—as this book will continually point out—charged with and now starting to understand the practises of Wild Re-Creation™ and, as such, entering a point of 'evolution' ourselves in terms of mass care practises, then we must walk into these changes with an open mind and a willingness to try new things. Wild Re-Creation™ is not only possible for all species but is nowhere near as difficult to start or maintain as one may assume.

Collating as much information as possible regarding a species and consistently maintaining this learning over the life of the collection, and then implementing any pertinent changes in a safe and measured way, is all that is required. Of course, there will be much debate and many practise changes over the ensuing years but, on the whole, these changes will be not only positive but also fairly easy to maintain and to grow upon from today onwards.

It is in the heart of the word 'evolution' that we, as keepers, must remain fixated. By this, I do not necessarily mean the 'Theory of Evolution' as in one species changing to another, but rather the 'evolution' of the hobby. The slow and moderated, overall positive change of practise that will allow every keeper to not only enjoy their animals as we should, but will indeed provide everything possible that is needed to allow every species to truly flourish in captive collections as they would in the wild. These are the modern ethics of our hobby, and the 'Forward-Thinking Reptile Keeper' will not only embrace these emerging theories but also will proactively enact their own research and then implement any changes according to their research in a safe and measured way. Practises that are ineffective or can be simplified will be dropped or altered, whilst practises that are positive will be ever expanded upon. This is the 'evolution' of our hobby. Ever-changing and ever Forward-Thinking.

Yes, Wild Re-Creation™ indeed is possible. Yes, Wild Re-Creation™ is beneficial. And yes, Wild Re-Creation™ is the direction towards which ethical trade/hobby is moving. It is of course made vastly easier with the invention of and availability of good science-based new product; it is only hampered by those that are unwilling to see these benefits and refuse to then implement these many varied possibilities of positive measures, adjustments and change into their systems—or even product ranges.

As we continue to change and adapt, the whole process will become ever easier: the old will make way for an ever-improving new and, as it does so, we will see fewer instances of avoidable disease, including Metabolic Bone Disorder (MBD) and many of the other nutritional deficiencies, as well as less early fatality and more and more positively stimulated, long-lived and reproductively positive animals that can and do reproduce without detriment to their own core biology.

The most important and fundamental aspect of this new way of thinking is to maintain an open and honest system of knowledge-sharing; a willing coming together as keepers with the sole aim of improving captive standards throughout the whole world, to be a shining light, whiter than white, and with nothing to hide. As keepers, we have an obligation to share both the positives and the negatives that we will undoubtedly encounter as we continue to grow and to expand our own personal and collective knowledge base. The advent of the internet greatly assists with this process of learning and knowledge-sharing, but of course, in and of itself, poses a risk with regards the proliferation of untested theory and practise. Accordingly, multiple sources of information must be sought out and even explained to a good reptile-focused vet before full implementation. Essentially, we are looking for a measured, worldwide positive change here, as such unproven tech or unheard of products must be proven safe before being introduced into our systems and/or animals. (As an example, I once saw on an internet auction site a seller recommending that reptile-keepers place their hand underneath one of his lamps. If the hand became red (dermal burn), then the lamp was still working and did not need to be changed. I do not have to tell you

"Bumblebee Walking Toad"

not only how inaccurate a measurement technique this is but how potentially dangerous it is to human life!)

Overall, risks and dangers will be exposed, and successes and triumphs will be shared and learnt with the simple press of a key. You never know: the very process of researching the care required for your pets may help to open your eyes to your own 'wild' needs and, as such, open an interesting window into your own, hopefully ever-improving human wellbeing. One thing is for sure: if you can understand your own Microbiome and start to understand the interactions and effects of what goes on inside of you after parameters change around you, you will start to see the whole of biology in a new and vastly more accurate way.

We are racing full steam ahead now into a new age of greatly improved exotic pet care. Never before have we had access to such a variety and depth of care-providing product and at such great prices. So why, then, when there is such choice, do some keepers still have welfare-related struggles within their own collections? Why do we still see worrying levels of MBD and shedding issues? Why do we not see common species (that is, some species that are abundant in the wild) reproduce consistently? And why do we still see animals living in less than ideal surroundings?

Well, the first thing I must point out is that we are dealing with core biology. Biological function cannot be overridden, influenced to change or be taken for granted. We cannot for one second pretend that we know more than nature or seek to second-guess her. No, I have said it before and it is a statement that I will live and die by: 'All of the secrets of great animal care are hidden in the wild animal'. It is this dedication to and the ongoing implementation of Wild Re-Creation™ that we will find all of the long-term answers to the frustrations we now encounter, including Metabolic Bone

Disorder, broad spectrum metabolic disorders, shedding issues, reproductive issues, short lifespan, skin/mouth rot, fatty liver disease, obesity, lethargy, stomatitis and anorexia.

As responsible keepers, we have the opportunity each and every day to positively chip away at these many and varied historical problems. It is upon ourselves that our animals depend daily, and it is—or should be—with us that they find the thoughtful and exact provision of their biological needs and processes. Of course, there are many 'dis-eases' that effect captive exotics, and some cannot be avoided (there will always be the frustrations and limitations of genetic variance, for example), but many of the old issues are simply owing to a poor understanding of reptilian biology and a poor or slow implementation of a series of positive changes. If we really are the experts, then surely we have a responsibility to keep up-to-date with as much of this emerging science and thinking as possible, and to then pass on what we have learned to our fellow keepers so that they can enjoy caring for their animals in the very best possible way for many years to come.

In order for positive change to occur, we have to be proactive with regard to making these changes ourselves. We have to have live displays that both cater to the core biological needs of our chosen species and which can be, at the same time, aesthetically pleasing.

These systems then can help to enthuse and inspire, and will show potential new keepers just how easy these new methods of care are. We then can use them to explain why these changes are so important and what we may expect from measure-improvement in the ensuing years. There are no real gains to be made if we do not understand or cannot explain the 'why' behind our actions when asked. These changes and the practise of knowledge-sharing will lead to better welfare, less chance of disease and a greatly increased level of success with regards captive breeding. We have to 'be the change' in the truest sense of the word. We lead by example and our examples should be good.

We should realise that it is with this theory of Wild Re-Creation™ that the next great period of growth in the hobby is waiting. When I say 'growth', I refer to both important areas of change:

1. Availability of truly captive-bred species
2. Biological understanding.

As an example, Bio-Activity is no longer just a theory as it was even 18 months ago, but is now being incorporated into pretty much every shop and private collection that I now visit—and done so in a realistic and workable way. The hobby-wide shift away from petrochemical-based fake plants and decoration is one that I once never thought at all possible, but now we see more and more shops going back to live plants and natural stone, which are both vastly safer and more effective in terms of long-term care. Alongside this, we are now starting to see a possible link between heated plastics and worrying VOC release: combine this release of potentially toxic compounds with poor ventilation and high temperatures, and we may have some real issues.

Change is afoot, and may it continue to help us to provide the very best level of care and support to our captive charges in this safe and measured way. It is only then that forward-thinking reptile-keeping becomes ethical and effective for everyone.

"Ornate Uromastyx"

Safety and Limitations to the Theory

Before we go any further, we must, as always, be very open and honest with ourselves. To every positive, there always will be a level of realistic limitation; most of these limitations can be safely worked around, but some simply cannot. It is by realising these limitations and finding any suitable and safe workarounds that we will step forward, with eyes wide open, into the next generation of ethical reptile-keeping.

We are, as a hobby, coming out of the stark 'sterile' days and running full steam ahead into this huge change towards Wild Re-Creation™ through Bio-Activity. On the whole—and for many of us—this will be an enjoyable and very positive change that will lead to many positive impacts on the health and continued wellbeing of our pets, and which should, in time, lead to better captive-breeding results through numbers of viable young, and without continuing detriment to the health of the females in our care. We must remember that an animal will seek to reproduce; this, in a sense, is its only goal in life, with many females laying eggs or giving birth almost continually (unless vet care is given) and to the wholesale depletion of any stored fats and minerals in her body. Yes, females can be literally bred to death. Young enter the world weak and, in some cases, go on into less than perfect systems from where they are bred, and the cycle of ever-decreasing health and wellbeing continues. What we need, as dedicated keepers and breeders, are fit, strong, genetically diverse, mineral-rich animals that will propel strength into as many generations as possible. In this way, we will see ever continued improvements in size, colour and organ function as we 'breed' strength back into our captive stocks and then energise them in an effective way.

As always, there will be a flip side or limitation to every potential positive move. A good period of thinking and advice-seeking will always be needed, to which informed choices must be implemented and maintained. Animals that are suffering with an increased or problematic parasitical load, as an example, would do nothing more than spread the infection throughout the enclosure through their faecal matter and, as such, keep re-infecting itself and any other enclosure mates, even after a period of treatment. Snakes with problematic mites also may be harder to treat in live systems (however, there is now anecdotal evidence to suggest that springtails and other custodians deal with this issue in-situ by consuming mite eggs—yet to be proven but well worth continued

"Mating Eyed lizards at Arcadia Reptile HQ"

debate), and of course we now have good access to predatory mites that can be introduced into the environment in which they will hunt down and consume the offending blood-sucking snake mites whilst they remain and then simply die off when no more are left to eat.

We also have an increased risk of respiratory tract infection in those animals that are prone to or that have suffered a weakening of the respiratory tract through persistent infection, genetic weakness or from what I now believe is exposure to Volatile Organic Compounds (VOC) produced from heated plastics. Poor air circulation also is viewed as a contributing factor here through humidity stagnation and prolific bacterial build-up in these rather hot, wet environments. There also is a risk of viral and/or bacterial infection from an infected animal to any enclosure mates. We also have to factor in a risk of subordinate animals not being allowed access to basking and/or food and water sources from a more dominant animal. Social hierarchy (territory and social position) and its ongoing maintenance in captive reptiles is both a profound and complex set of comprising actions and communication, and therefore should not be underestimated and should be permitted to play a pivotal role in enclosure design, decoration, group size and in sex ratio.

All of these 'risks' or limitations only remain as such if they are not thoughtfully, properly and proactively managed. In most cases,

In each case, we should seek the advice of a good reptile-focused vet and then make informed choices about the pertinent long-term care of the individual animal or animals that are in our care."

many of these limitations can be overcome quite simply over time, and the animal allowed to benefit in full from the bulk of the theory. In other cases, the animal is simply too sick or at too high a risk to be allowed access to this kind of continued husbandry. In each case, we should seek the advice of a good reptile-focused vet and then make informed choices about the pertinent long-term care of the individual animal or animals that are in our care.

Parasitical load, for example, now can be treated quite easily, either by chemical or herbal remedy. This method of treatment is both largely safe and is measurable (alongside the advice of a reptile-focused vet). As a point of reference, it can be easily monitored with simple microscopy, now via a quick and affordable and fairly easy to understand postal service. Any infection then can be treated on an ongoing basis and as required for your own species. In cases where parasitical load is suddenly raised and therefore requires a sudden or unexplained re-treatment, the entire system may need to be started once again. (Look at the environmental conditions and stressors here; many cases of a sudden parasitical infection are born from a lowering of useful gut flora after a period of great stress or other underlying illness. Has the animal been moved? Has the enclosure been altered? Are there any environmental changes in or around the viv or has an enclosure mate been bullying it?) A product such as Verm-X can be used for just three days each month to ensure effective gut health and to help eliminate the risk of parasites recurring. Again, seek good veterinary advice first and accurately follow brand instructions.

For those individual animals that may have a weakened respiratory system or that are historically prone to chronic respiratory infection advice must be sought by a reptile-focused vet before any changes to the animal's care are made. It even may be better for that particular animal to be continued to be kept in sterile and easy-to-clean and monitor surroundings, especially if it requires regular nebulised treatment. In each and every case, we must remain focussed on animal welfare; this is our joint top priority and guiding force.

In a similar way, those animals that may have a level of disease or have come from rescues in a poor state or have been born with a genetic defect that would limit good self-regulation, advice must be sought and Bio-Activity avoided until proven safe for that particular animal. (Again, there is anecdotal evidence here of some snakes with breathing issues being almost miraculously cured when placed into a Bio-Active system; however, this is yet to be proven and may simply be an outworking of a higher level of ambient humidity and/or its release from any potential VOC exposure when not tubbed, again not proven but worth debating.) We must view this implementation as a case-by-case project and seek to overcome as many negatives as possible. As always, there will be individual animals or even animal groups that are simply not suited to the method.

Newly acquired animals from all sources must be permitted a period of safe and well-maintained quarantine before being introduced to a Bio-Active system, regardless of whether or not it has live animals inside of it. We must not rely on the local shops and traders to have carried out this rather lengthy job first. Keep good written records (Excel can help greatly with this) and prove to yourself that every aspect of animal care/health has been checked and has/can be catered for. We, as keepers, will indeed need time to assess the health and wellbeing of each and every animal, and we will need to set time aside to treat any ongoing condition first. When the animal is settled and feeding and has been proven to be healthy and to not pose a parasite risk, it then can be introduced into the system where it will surely go on to thrive.

The watchword here is to double-check everything—at all times. If you have an uneasy feeling about your animal, see your reptile specialist vet without delay. Ask other keepers, of course, and read books and watch videos, but back-up this at home research with medical proof. Early intervention with regards to infection and/or disease is far more effective in terms of finding a lasting cure or repair, and will save you lots of money in vet's fees going forward than waiting to see what will happen over time, as that is quite plain to see: the animal may continue to degrade and become unwell and may require longer, deeper and more expensive treatment. Animal welfare must be at the top of our list at all times. Good record-keeping will help in this, and will enable your vet to provide the exact care that is required for your species in the home that you have provided for it.

I place great importance on this. As such, I will cover this subject once again from a different angle later on in the book.

Measuring UVB

You will see me state many times throughout this book of theories and advice that we should never add anything into our enclosures or into the care parameters of the species that we keep if it is not;

A. Proven to be safe, and
B. cannot be measured accurately.

These are the checks and balances needed to be sure that we are doing as much as possible to secure the effective wellbeing of our pets in the safest and most balanced way possible. For instance, if we were to add a new supplement or dietary addition into the diets of our pets, we must know that the correct scientific work has been done beforehand to prove that every ingredient is not only safe to use, but does not have an unhelpful interaction with other ingredients or external parameters. Doses should be stated for potentially toxic compounds and advice given so as to mitigate or otherwise treat any accidental oversupply. (Exposure to Heat, light, UV, water, O_2 and any other element can change the actions and/or potency of any other element over time.)

In terms of measuring UVB energy, currently, there is only one device that is available to consumers that I personally would trust to provide me with not only an accurate but a usable quantification of solar energy. This meter is called the Solarmeter 6.5.

The Solarmeter 6.5 measures the total quantity of UV and shows this as a numerical value. We refer to this value or quantity as the 'UV Index' or 'Solar Index'. This is the same measurement that you will see on modern weather reports, and directly relates to the amount of energy available in a location—in our case, a habitat.

One very positive thing about the 6.5 is that it can be taken to an animal's home nation and used to measure direct levels of UV energy where any given species is found. We then can use the same device to re-create the required index per species underneath artificial UVB projection lamps. This is the only metre of which I am aware that can do this both accurately and with ease.

Solarmeters are very easy to use: simply point the photosensitive cell at the light source and press the button that is central to the

> There is only one device that is available to consumers that I personally would trust to provide me with not only an accurate but a usable quantification of solar energy. This metre is called the Solarmeter 6.5."

metre; this will provide an instant readout. Make a note of this. Take 5 readings per location and take an average between them all to be sure of the exact index output. It is surprising how much of a variance can be measured under a lamp, particularly with the subtle movements of the hand and angle of measurement.

These meters usually come in a protective case, but I find it good practise to clean the sensor with a spectacle cleaning cloth just to be sure of the most accurate reading.

These devices are not cheap to buy, but not only will they provide an insight into the true power of the sun and its spread in any given habitat, and thus enable you to accurately re-create this in the home, but it also will show you the continued potent lifespan of your UVB system at any given moment.

"Solarmeter 6.5 in use"

Solar Pathways

The three diagrams overleaf clearly show the natural pathway of sunlight through the atmosphere and onto/into the planet; this is how light, and energy from light, reaches us under the protective layer of atmosphere and, as you will see, it is not as a simple a process as one may think. The sun sustains us and has done throughout our history: it is with the intricacies of sunlight and its knock-on effects with regard to sustaining life that we need to spend some time. If we can understand that terrestrial light does not just travel from the sun to the earth and then magically disappear, then we are already half way to designing fully functioning systems of Wild Re-Creation™.

These images clearly show light as a full-spectrum solar source entering a range of ecosystems, and how this energy then further travels around the eco system, and how the species that may live in that habitat may make use of it in the safest and most efficient way. Seeing these solar pathways in a simple pictorial form helps us to understand the relationships that all species, including our own and also the other more crepuscular and arboreal species, have with the sun. It is my aim to accurately describe just how

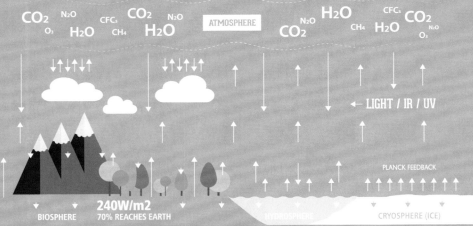

340W/m2
30% REFLECTED BACK UPWARDS

INFRARED=HEAT
UVC BLOCKED BY ATMOSPHERE
FULL SPECTRUM SUNLIGHT CONTAINS ALL TERRESTRIAL WAVELENGTHS.
WATER VAPOUR IS FANTASTIC (BLANKET) TRAPPING IN WARMTH.

ATMOSPHERE REDUCES STRONG SUN BUT INSULATES
HEAT IN LIKE A BLANKET.

1.

CO_2 N_2O CFCs CO_2 N_2O ATMOSPHERE N_2O H_2O CFCs CO_2
O_3 H_2O CH_4 H_2O CO_2 CH_4 H_2O N_2O O_3

← LIGHT / IR / UV

PLANCK FEEDBACK

240W/m2
BIOSPHERE 70% REACHES EARTH HYDROSPHERE CRYOSPHERE (ICE)

The safe transference of solar energy into our world is of course the driving force that sustains all life forms.

This diagram shows the pathway of light as it is produced from the sun and travels down towards the earth crust, seas and ice. Light does not travel in straight lines and then disappear, no it is reflected in countless ways, each reflection carrying a % of the energy of light being UV and I.R as it travels.

It is now becoming obvious that I-R and UV energy of both terrestrial groups of wavelengths can be reflected and utilised by the earth's inhabitants in almost miraculous ways.

The ability to see many of the wavelengths via Tetrachromacy of course is a useful tool with regard to self-regulation. This also shows how heat (I.R) and UV can reflect back upwards off of the floor and towards the underside of a species.

It also shows stored heat in the soil and rocks as it is re-emitted back into the habitat. This safe form of belly warmth is essential for the effective function of internal organs and core processes like digestion.

For more information visit our website
www.arcadia-reptile.com
email: arcadiareptile@arcadia-uk.com

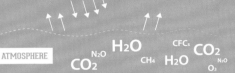

2

CO_2 N_2O CFC_s CO_2 N_2O ATMOSPHERE N_2O H_2O CFC_s CO_2

O_3 H_2O CH_4 H_2O CO_2 CH_4 H_2O N_2O O_3

LIGHT / IR / UVA/B

ARID TERRAIN

This diagram shows the basic pathway of light from the sun, how it is reflected back into the localised environment in a myriad of angles and off of most things that it encounters.

This is the process that allows the effective transference of light and its energy (UV/I-R) back off of the floor and rocks and into porous rocks and burrow mouths where some species will rest away from searing heat and predation by day.

This is a prime example of how a crepuscular species from arid/scrubland terrain can still benefit in full from both heat, being I-R and UVA-B. We call this "rock-scatter illumination".

3

CO_2 N_2O CFC_s CO_2 N_2O ATMOSPHERE N_2O H_2O CFC_s CO_2

O_3 H_2O CH_4 H_2O CO_2 CH_4 H_2O O_3

LIGHT / IR / UVA/B

JUNGLE

This diagram shows the basic pathway of light from the sun, how it is absorbed and reflected by water, leaves and rocks in the forest/jungle habitats of the world.

An arboreal species will benefit from exposure to direct sunlight from the top down but they would also be benefiting from light as it bounces around the canopy and down into the understory and further still towards the forest floor.

Again nocturnes that maybe found asleep by day and crepuscular species that are more active in lower light levels will still be able to benefit from this broad scatter of light as it travels at many angles through a forest. We call this "leaf-scatter illumination".

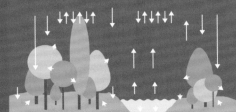

both 'rock' and 'leaf' scatter illumination have an active and vital role in the health and wellbeing of all species, irrespective of their position in the ecosystem.

If we, as keepers, can realise that sunlight does not just travel down from the sun in straight lines and hit the back and the head of a species or then magically disappear, we will start to truly understand the actions and limitations of light projections for any given species. Light, in its 'full spectrum', bounces around almost eternally under the atmosphere and around every other item that it encounters (rock, water, leaves, soil, ice, etc.), decreasing in power very slowly but infiltrating every nook and cranny or gap in the forest, desert or savannah; this is how the thinner skinned/crepuscular species are able to obtain this essential solar energy and make full use of the D3 cycle in the wild, even when not 'openly full-body basking'. Why expose the whole body when you can develop a thinner more light-penetrating skin and simply expose a leg or a foot or the tail and then come out fully in safer, lower light times? Openly basking for many species simply increases the risk of predation. It would make evolutionary sense for a species to hide away in porous rocks and burrows or to stay hidden on the sides of trees and bushes or to sit sleeping under leaves and to still be able to benefit from a percentage of this reflected sunlight, however small, from the direct solar source or as it continues to bounce around the whole habitat.

'To test this theory in the home is fairly easy. Obtain a small sheet of thick black card and a normal torch. Safely poke around 12-15 holes randomly into the surface of the card with a fairly thick pin. The holes should be around 1mm thick. Then stick or hold the card with holes in front of the torch in a dark room. Shine the torch at a wall and see the columns of light as they project against the surface. This is the same way that columns of light travel around an environment and are made available to the animals'.

This process encompasses the entire full-spectrum of sunlight from UVB to long wavelength infra-red. We can now start to understand how all of the terrestrial wavelengths of light effect the environment and how the animals living there can make a safe and effective use of them. We can see how this infra-red or heat is not only stored in part (by rocks and high-density materials) but also is reflected back into the habitat—heat is infra-red, a wavelength of light. This process greatly benefits many species as it reflects back upwards towards the belly and all around the animal. I mentioned in my last book, 'The Arcadia Guide to Reptile and Amphibian Nutrition', just how vital heat is to the process of digestion and gastrointestinal transit, and how many cases of captive impaction can be attributed not only to a poor choice of substrate but also to poor or inadequate hydration and poorly appropriated heat. This natural process of heat being stored and reflected not only helps to heat and to regulate the core temperature of an ectothermic species, but also becomes an aid to its own core biological processes, including internal organ function and digestion. We must also accept that the weaker wavelengths of light, including UVB, act in largely the same way as they reflect off of the locality and into the surrounding habitat— of course being made available to all in some way as they travel.

The sun produces all of the wavelengths of light from X-ray to Microwave. Many of these wavelengths are blocked by the earth's atmosphere, including deadly UVC. Approximately 30% of the sun's power is reflected back off of our atmosphere/ozone layer and back into space.

The atmosphere is made of so-called 'greenhouse gases'. These gases act as an essential layer or blanket around the earth, which shields us from the sun's dangerous wavelengths whilst also acting to protect us from extreme weather. These gases really do act like a blanket that keeps both heat and water-vapour in (like a greenhouse). This 'blanket' acts as a filter, blocking out harmful radiation but allowing UVA, UVB, visible light and I-R through.

UVB, UVA, visible light and long- and short-wavelength infra-red pass through the atmosphere as a percentage of light. This terrestrial light travels downwards and at a multitude of angles. Some of this energy then is reflected back up into the terrestrial atmosphere by the clouds, where it can continue to bounce around. A percentage reflects around the earth's terrain to be stored as heat by the ecosystem before being released back into the eco-system once again.

'Remember those experiments at school where you would shine a beam of light through a prism? Well this is just exposing the prismatic effect. The whole range of colours of light are split and spread through colour aberration in the prism, which allows you to see how light is broken down into its individual colour component. This is exactly the same with the sun: the sun is not yellow or just a source of heat and light, but rather is made up from every one of these colours or wavelengths. Place a prism in a beam of sunlight to see this for yourself.'

The Biosphere (living earth/plants/soil/rocks, etc.), hydrosphere (water) and cryosphere (ice) all reflect this light and the energy from light back into the ecosystem in differing amounts, according to their nature. The earth and its water sources store large quantities of the energy/heat, which then can be used and/or re-

released. Ice, however, reflects the majority of this energy back around the atmosphere; this is referred to as the earth's Albedo/ Planck feedback.

The atmosphere or ozone layer is made up from many gases, some of which are or have become problematic, but it is true to say that most are essential to our survival. It is when these gases are altered 'by man', out of proportion, that an imbalance occurs and that we can enter periods of 'non-natural global warming'. This, of course, is due to the prevalence—and over-production, in our case—of CO_2 which is now at a record 400–450 ppm. This count is still currently increasing and remains extremely worrying!

(What happens if our impact upon the climate of the earth causes a permanent change where indexes increase above and beyond the levels of which a reptile has developed protection against and for which they have a use? Will the animals adapt to their ecosystem and hide away more as to seek protection or will we see a level of cellular change or dermal thickening in a quicker period of time than we currently assume is needed? Or alternatively will we start to see a localised extinction that goes on to spread? At this stage, nobody really knows; regardless, however, there is an important principle hidden here that must be kept in mind and that I will be sure to remind you of throughout this book: reptiles change and

"Natural stone and organic soil"

adapt slowly. We have, in this case, apparently actioned a planet-wide potential disaster that could have a very negative impact on all life. This scenario would replicate a keeper overproviding a solar index without providing an area in which an animal can self-regulate properly in captivity, meaning only bad things will happen.)

Here are some of the essential atmospherically occurring gases that make up our protective and insulating ozone layer. Water (H_2O), of course, is the most prevalent gas, and is most essential for the continuation of life in more ways than one.

$H2O, O_3, N_2O, CH_4, CFCs, CO_2.$

If we can truly understand light and its pathway all around us, as well as its uses and limitations in biology, we will be able to generate the most accurate and effective systems of Wild Re-Creation™ inside of our own enclosures. The ever-increasing quantity of science available to us really does enable us, as Forward-thinking Reptile keepers, to constantly improve our care systems through well placed and well thought-out change.

Darkness

We, as modern and educated keepers, must realise that all nature is indicative! Every part of its 'web' of knowledge will provide us with vital clues towards effective animal care provision. Likewise, every part of nature is and should be a valuable learning experience for us all, regardless of the species or even group that we keep, whether flora or fauna. As we are now starting to see, light and energy from light (light is energy) is as vital to all 'life' as is food and water, more so for ectothermic animals as they would not have the levels of energy required to even find food or water without this 'light'. The opposite of this provision of light and energy from light is, of course, darkness. So, if a species has adapted/evolved to utilise light in all of its terrestrial wavelengths—that is, to use light as a tool or function so that it can thrive in its own local area—will it have developed a use for a lack of light?

The answer to this question, of course, is an emphatic yes! In fact, and in a very real sense, the provision of darkness is just as important to the core biological cycles of reptiles (most lifeforms) as periods of natural sunlight is. Even if we forget for a moment those very truly, rare nocturnal species, or even those more common crepuscular animals, darkness is a time in which the core biological processes of a reptile (animal and plant) starts to allow the exact and effective assimilation of food and the utilisation of the vitamins and minerals that have been collected during the more active period. As I pointed out in my book about 'MBD', a period of darkness is vital to maintaining the D3 cycle as a whole and ensuring its continued potency.

Rest is vital. Maintaining a system in which light is provided for all through the night, even in quite small amounts, cannot only interfere with an animal's biological cycles but can have a negative impact upon core brain function and even reproduction. Therefore, we must be sure of the correct provision of darkness alongside light. We should refrain from using light-emitting heat sources throughout the night, and the use of low lux blue moon LED systems (440–480 nm) should only be used as a lenticular lensed 'flood' source for crepuscular viewing in the evening and then must be switched off for the majority of the night. With regard to these low-energy LED moonlight systems, I suggest that 2 hours' use after the main lighting has been switched off would replicate lower light levels before the provision of total darkness and therefore would be safe.

"Wonder Gecko"

We also should place great importance on the provision of water through humidity in the early morning and, of course, evening/ leading into the night. A light spray down just before an animal settles down for the night could make the difference between adequate hydration and excellent hydration and, of course, is part of Wild Re-Creation™ for all species, not only those that hail from the forests and jungles. Humidity (that is airborne water) is a vital tool from which reptiles (most animals, actually) can top-up on gathered water levels while they rest; this therefore can be considered as most important. Even in the most arid regions, air humidity can go up surprisingly in the evening and morning, or be obtained underground in the burrows as the animal rests.

Light and its calculated omission, of course, also can be used to replicate seasonality, both in terms of an increase of food and light, leading to growth and reproduction, and its decrease leading to brumation in those species that require it. This is well-known in farming, where light levels are used to lengthen breeding cycles or otherwise increase yield in poultry. Even canary and budgerigar breeders will use full-spectrum lighting to lengthen the day and start the breeding season early. Yes, light is all important to life in all of its terrestrial wavelengths. To boost the efficacy of our care programmes and light provision systems, we must ensure that we view this provision of total darkness as just as important as providing light.

Maintaining wild-like Circadian rhythms at all times is not a luxury or optional extra for keepers in deciding whether to implement. They are indeed part of the developed state of the species that we keep; as such, we must view the correct provision of these rhythms as core to our animals biological needs.

Solar Indexes from Around the World

I n my mind, it is the ever-evolving relationship between good science and vastly improved technology that holds the key to the next wave of improvements for captive exotic animals. If we, as keepers, , as I have stated already and will continue to do so, can implement these things in a timely manner, we will see fewer occurrence of avoidable disease, and we will; further witness longer, healthier lives and benefits from dedicated species-specific enrichment and, therefore, better reproductive and survival rates going forward.

"Captive Bred Golden Mantella froglet at Arcadia Reptile HQ"

One of the ways in which we can work smartly to provide any given species with everything that it requires to thrive of course is to offer a dedicated and measured area of enclosure in which the animal can choose to obtain the average wild solar index or 'quantity' of UVB that is common to that species. Of course, every species uses sunlight in a different way: some are nocturnal, some crepuscular and some diurnal, some are terrestrial, and some arboreal and, of course, every variation in between. Yes, every species is different, and each has an amazing way of taking every possible thing it needs from its own environment and giving back into this environment in its own way. We have to factor in many things in order to be truly forward-thinking. We need to factor in the way that light travels to a species and then what would happen to this light and, of course, the evolutionary requirements of the species with regards to light. We have to look at leaf or rock scatter light patterns, reflections back from the earth itself, stone (stone mass/density and colour), water and, of course, limiting actions, such as predator avoidance, which, in itself, is a driving force behind 'solar utilisation' and self-regulation.

In truth, due to the progressive nature of science and technology, the theory of providing these parameters must remain fluid as we continue to learn more and more each and every day. There are no hard and fast correct answers, and nor should there ever be: if we pretend that we 'know it all', we stray from the goals of 'forward-thinking reptile-keeping'. It therefore is up to each and every keeper to keep up-to-date with advances in technology and with the current waves of scientific thought, and we must be willing to make slight or even great adjustments as these new theories emerge. In this way, we will be ever-evolving ourselves with regard to our care practises.

One of the key life-support parameters of reptile care is, of course, the correct provision of UVB as part of full-spectrum, plus UVB lighting. In order to be truly 'forward-thinking'—and to be sure that we are providing all that a species needs, we should seek to provide the average quantity of energy from light (UVindex) per species, per enclosure, in a safe and MEASURED way. This should also incorporate the core values of the light and shade method so as to allow for effective self-regulation between these columns or defined areas of energy. We then will, by definition, be providing the core, evolved biological parameters of any given species in terms of their solar energy requirements.

It is important that we do not blast irradiate or over-expose a species to a level/index of energy for which it does not use, nor has access to in the wild, as this could represent a chronic oversupply of this energy above and beyond its own evolved level

"Madagascan Ground or Ocelot Gecko"

of protection from the sun. We should, however, seek to provide the upper index or greatest quantity of solar energy that is common to a species in its habitat and to then allow that species to choose where and when to obtain the correct level for them as and when they choose to and in line with their biological needs. These highly advanced animals can then be kept well and to their own particular wild environmental parameters, but we must be sure that we then balance this level of basking exposure with a well thought-out depreciation into cool and shade, as per the light and shade method. Importantly, this then would allow for the safe, self-regulation to the 'wild' or given 'required' level of your particular animal on that particular day. The animal, whatever species, then can use the energy that you have provided in line with its own needs and in the way it is intended. This, of course, might involve be full body exposure or exposure to a part of the body, just the tip of the tail or a foot, or even exposure to reflected energy to the softer sides and underside of the body while it rests semi-hidden behind the decoration.

If we understand the basic principles of UV energy and its pathways and the limitations to these terrestrial wavelengths, we then will become equipped to provide exactly what is needed in this safe and, of course, measured way. We must, however, ensure the completion of some in-depth research into the wild species, active periods, elevation in the environment, etc.; we then can use this priceless information to engineer, within our enclosures, these very effective systems that will allow this wild level of exposure. Thoughtful decoration, of course, is vital for this method to succeed. We should never hang lamps low down into vivs, for instance, just to provide the animal with greater power: all this does is increase the risk of ocular infection; rather, it is better to fit lamps above the animal and to then use rocks, plants and branches so that the species can climb upwards towards the lamp when and if it has need.

In reality, the index of solar energy at the floor of many rainforests, particularly owing to the 'leaf scatter patterns' described, can still be very high indeed—higher than we currently think—but, of course, these higher potency areas will be limited to a myriad of shafts of energy rather than huge patches or 'floods' of light. In this way, self-regulation is a very simple process. Consider the projections of light from a glitter ball and you will be some way to understanding what I mean.

It is vital that we, as forward-thinking keepers, realise that, just because a deeply shaded area of Costa Rica may only provide an index of 0.25-0.5 at the forest floor, that this is not the 'total' amount of energy available to a species in its whole range. No, the benefit of the theory of leaf scatter in itself will dictate that many thin shafts of light at greater indexes will push through the canopy and down into the understory and towards the forest floor, either from the direct source or via a myriad of reflection. These animals then can use these thin shafts as and when they have need. We could, if it is easier, view them as tiny 'tanning salons'; provided for by nature and used by the animal to thrive. We must also keep in mind that almost all species can climb to some degree, although some may be better than others. (Many of the species that we keep and have been told are ground dwellers are actually quite often found climbing up trees and bushes or travelling to higher elevations in their habitats both daily and/or in season. The bearded dragon, corn snake, royal python and leopard gecko, for example, all have been found doing this, and will readily climb inside of our enclosures.) This, in itself, will greatly increase the variation and quantity of index available to the species. Even an elevation of 5' from the forest floor will show a potential 3x increase in the available power and sheer footprint of light.

In real terms, we will need to factor into our choice of lamp provision the style and density of decoration of each and every vivarium that we own. We could make rather general assumptions per species, 6% UVB for such a species, and 12% for another. In reality, however, UVB significantly decreases in potency the further the light has to travel from a lamp. It is entirely possible that a high output T5 12% UVB reptile lamp could be used over an enclosure of Dendrobates, but only if the enclosure was high enough to require such a level of energy to be pushed down towards the floor where the frogs would spend the majority of their time. So what should we do? As I have already pointed out, we simply need to use a metre to measure and to plot out the areas of energy that we provide. Everything that we add into the

> As forward-thinking keepers, it is vital that we are fully aware of the weather patterns and seasonal patterns of the species we keep."

lives of our pets should be safe, and it must be measurable or we should not seek to provide for it.

As a rule of thumb, and for the most commonly kept deep-forest or crepuscular species, we could provide an index of 1–3 depending on the need and behaviour of a species and its elevation above sea level in the home range at 'basking'. If we provide this level or index of energy for these leaf litter or crepuscular animals at a formal 'basking' zone, we will not go far wrong. This, in itself, is both Safe and Measurable as the animal, or animals, will be able to self-regulate into full exposure and away into total shade, and of course can utilise the myriad of subtle index changes in-between.

As forward-thinking keepers, it is vital that we are fully aware of the weather patterns and seasonal patterns of the species we keep. As I have pointed out, there is no real 'magic bullet' in terms of artificial solar replication; therefore, we must use wild data within the limitations of the technology available to us. We then can use this data to make provision for our own animals. In many cases, the level of energy or index in the home ranges is far greater than we realise. It is important that we take a detailed look at this information and look over a long period of time, and that we allow for the negative results of climate change.

"Dwarf Chameleon from Cameroon"

(I see this each day within our own collections. Let's take the Madagascan Plated lizard, *Zonosaurus madagascarensis*, as an example. If you look at anecdotal evidence, you could surmise that this is a deep-forest and scrubland species that spends its days rummaging around in the mud, under the leaf litter, and, as such, would not have a use for high levels of sunlight, meaning a low percentage or output UVB system may be advised. In reality, however, the solar index off of the coast of Africa is huge. Light travels well and continues to bounce around the terrain. In reality, this species can easily obtain and use through self-regulation indexes of over 7 throughout much of the day. Couple this with the quite obvious thicker scales across the animal's back and you can see that they do indeed have a use for and an interaction with the sun at this higher level or they would not have developed the thicker scales in the first place. Our collection here has access to a solar gradient from 0.00 at the far cool side and, of course, under the deep Bio-Active substrate, right the way up to 8.50 at the top of the highest basking/climbing branch. Each and every day, each animal in the trio will take it in turns to climb up to this highest branch, lay out flat, and willingly expose itself to this level of upper index basking for around 30–40 minutes. They then get on with the day's business of rooting around, hunting and hopefully mating, all the while utilising the vast array of solar indexes that are available to them. Our experience is positive: not only are the animals growing well but they also are displaying a deep and rich level of colouration and have produced, incubated and hatched in-situ, a number of viable young in the first season; they have not only survived but are truly thriving in their own right. We believe that this is the first documented case of this species being truly captive-bred and the young successfully raised. We copied the wild and the wild paid us back.)

"Madagascan Plated Lizard at Arcadia Reptile HQ"

To put this theory into perspective, the MET shows the total index in the UK as 1-2 in the south and 0-1 in the north in the early months of 2015. In the height of summer, we are exposed at midday to an index of around 5-7 in the south of the UK, which is much higher than it used to be even 5 years ago (climate change). In some cases, merely using the published index per environment could in itself cause a keeper to over provide for that species; that is, to provide a UVB system that generates an index above the level of evolved protection. Climate change is a very real risk to us all as indexes increase quicker than evolution allows a species to develop protection against. As such, we should, look at the average index per species and then round down to the next number.

Let's look at the indexes today from some of the world's biggest reptile-exporting nations or for commonly kept species (early-2015)

We can easily see the temp, cloud density, wind speed, humidity and UVI on online weather information resources. These readings, of course, will be taken in the towns and not in forests, but nevertheless it is a great place to start. We then use our species knowledge to make forward-thinking and intelligent choices about the energy we provide per target species.

Weather online shows;

Costa Rica today an index 10-12 which is about as high as it gets and would for almost all species be detrimental if dedicated shade provision was not supplied.

- Panama city is 7-8
- Kabul is 4-5 and it is Winter
- Tanzania is 11-12 (very high)
- Ghana is 6-7 at the coast, rising to 11-12 inland
- Benin is showing 40 degrees and an index of 10-11
- Togo is 38 degrees and showing an index range of 6-9
- Most of Vietnam is 10-11, but with some slightly lower indexes at the extremities of the land masses Jakarta is 8-11
- Miami is 22 degrees and raining, but still providing an index of 6-7
- Ilse de pins (from where the crested gecko originates) is 32 degrees and has an index of 7-9 today!

We therefore can see how reflected and refracted light can be utilised by these crepuscular species in a very efficient way. Even if the total energy depreciation as light bounces down through the trees removes two-thirds of the power, they still would be exposed to an index of 1-3. In real terms, an active and potent dose that can and will be used per species in the safest and most effective way possible. Remember; an animal does not have to be awake to benefit in full from the full power of the sun; they are more than able to sleep tucked away on the side of a tree during the day and to allow partial exposure from direct shafts or reflected columns of light. This will have exactly the same effect and process inside of them as it does for an openly-basking diurnal species. In a sense, they may be 'charging' during the day to sustain the evening and night-time's activity.

Outback Australia is showing a real spike in index—upwards of 10 at midday—and is listed as extreme. In reality, exposing a species without access to shade at this level would indeed and, in most cases, cause an oversupply heading towards negative genetic change at a dermal level at least. We would see that the diurnal species would have taken the energy needed earlier on in the day and would then retreat to the burrow at the strongest and most dangerous periods.

In Ambanja, Madagascar, it is raining heavily today, and for the next whole week, with heavy thunder and lightning storms. The temperature is at a high of 33 degrees, but still has a massive UV energy of 6-8! Sambava is hot and stormy also, but is showing an index of 12, which beggars belief. We then can see why the panther chameleons are so good at hiding under leaves and branches and, as such, removing themselves from direct exposure to these colossal amounts of power. We also can see why species like the Madagascan Iguanas and plated lizards have evolved such thick, armour-plated skin, and then can spend longer periods of time in full exposure in these high quantities.

So, we can see how we can use weather reports as a starting point for our own research. We cannot just use one day's weather, of course; we must look at the weather patterns per species over the whole year and over the past 10-20 years where such information occurs. We then can cross this info with home-nation species' guides; where is it found and at what time of day and in what type of habitat? We can then use this vital information to formulate a very educated guess at the safest level of power and accordingly seek to provide this level in a safe and measured way.

Does this information mean that we should blast our beardies all of the time and over the whole enclosure with super high indexes of 10-12? No! We have to also factor in climate change, day night cycles, season and, of course, wild behaviour. Desert species like these Agamids will typically dig into their burrows and hide during the searing heat of the day. An index of 6-7 at the very centre of basking is about as high as I would ever want to see used for a bearded dragon, but of course as part of a well-set system of light and shade. Yes, they can tolerate higher indexes, as shown by the wild weather patterns, but in order to do this they have a whole habitat to use— not just a 4x2x2 enclosure with a few rocks. To confirm once again, the basking area is the area of an enclosure where it is hottest and where the UVB index is greatest; this is where the distance between the lamp and the animals back is at the shortest point. The animal then has the choice of whether to allow full exposure and for how long, and to choose any of the thousands of variations downwards in power as it descends and moves throughout the enclosure.

We, as forward-thinking keepers, need to realise that each and every species has its own special relationship with its own individual habitat and within its own ecosystem. It therefore has changed and adapted over vast periods of time to take all that it needs from this ecosystem, ensuring it not only thrives in its own right but can continue to project its own genes as far into the future as possible, thus securing the survival of the species as a whole and its own bloodline far into the future.

If we learn from this vital wild information in as many parameters as possible, including earth and water mineral content, humidity, diet, light and so on, we will, by definition, be providing an ethical and effective environment in which they can live a full and enriched life.

I believe that it is this 'macro' level of in-depth research that holds the many keys to the next very significant leap in captive care techniques.

"Giant Day Gecko"

The Light and Shade Method Explained

The light and shade method is now widely accepted in professional Zoological collections and specialist stores, and recently has started to become the norm in 'at home' collections—and for good reason. The term 'the light and shade method' is used to describe the practice of grouping a measured heat and light source together over an equally measured and continuously measurable portion of an enclosure (no matter the size) and accordingly matching this section or basking zone with a graduated drop-off into a natural pattern of cool and shade.

To ensure that we are providing the correct quantity of light to a species, we first must look at the habitat and origin of the species that is to be accommodated. As stated, we have to glean our data from the country of origin to be precise with our captive provision. Ranger reports and weather pattern reports can be used from these islands to find an average UVI, length of daylight and temperature scale per environment. The keeper then will need to use wild activity data to decide on the position and activity of the species selected. Data, such as the length of time spent in shade or burrows, can be taken into account, and a maximum index decided upon. This data can be drilled down further for any species, subspecies and localities, i.e. elevation above sea level per locale, etc.

It is vital that the provision of light is at the forefront of enclosure design when using the light and shade method. Typically, we should aim to illuminate one-third to half of the total enclosure with a usable graduation of lighting, including UV. This will leave a very usable area of shade and decreasing temperatures that can be used by the species as the need arises. I am a firm believer that a species knows its own core needs and, if provided with access to a wild gradient, they will use this gradient to maintain effective thermoregulation and wild-like levels of biological change through this effective 'self-regulation'.

This method is dependent on a few basic core principles. Firstly, we must provide a light source that projects a footprint of light that is wide enough to provide energy to the total length of the body of the chosen species, minus the length of the tail at a minimum. The area of light containing UV can be bigger than the size of the body, of course, in very large enclosures, as long at the animal has the ability to self-regulate from the maximum

"Caiman Lizard"

wild index to total shade at any given time. This then allows the animal to choose its own level of power as it has need in all of its variations of power as light reflects and bounces around and trails off into shade.

For climbing and arboreal species, we must ensure that the species kept cannot obtain a dose of UV that is higher than can be found in the country of origin: it is at this level that any species will have evolved a level of protection against and may not be able to cope with indexes above this 'norm' when provided in a restricted environment. We can use our decoration skills to ensure this. In these cases, the light and shade method also can be invoked vertically; this will mean the highest heat and highest index found at the top of the enclosure, with these levels reducing towards the bottom of the enclosure. It therefore is vital that climbing places are not provided to a higher level per enclosure than that which provides the agreed maximum target index. This may be a good way of providing a level of energy for many of the chameleon, arboreal Agamids, varanids and, of course, snakes and amphibian species.

As a side note, which we will cover further later on in this book, it is well worth pointing out that a lighting system, regardless of its accuracy and potency, is only as good as the diet that is being used per species, and also if the level of hydration is adequate enough to allow for the completion of all of the biological functions required to make use of the nutrients on offer. A full and varied diet is essential to the effective and long-term care and propagation of captive exotics, as it is with every species, including our own. A one or two species live-food offering, even if gut-loaded, quite simply never can fulfil or even truly cater for the biological requirements and functions of most of the species that we keep. Very few predators only predate upon a single species or food type; even the snail-eaters will consume a wide variety of snail species, and we also must factor in the diet of the snail as this will have an effect upon the predator, as does the nutrition available to the plant. Importantly, it is all passed upwards and outwards as part of a fully functioning and potent food web.

As you can see, we quite plainly still continue to struggle to properly mimic a truly wild diet in a measured and accurate way. As such, we must continue to rely upon quality and well though-out supplementation. The key here is to ensure understanding of vitamin and mineral powders, how they work, their limitations and, of course, the positives and negatives of use. We must, as an example, realise that many of the commercial products will have some level of elemental change during and following exposure to air, light, water and UVB. These elemental changes are thought

> We must also realise that the effective provision of hydration in a format that any given species can make use of best is critical to the maintenance of the D3 cycle and all of its biological offshoots."

to make some components less potent and some become more aggressive. Time will tell, of course, as we research further and further into the actual needs of captive animals and the effects of the products available for them to use.

We must also realise that the effective provision of hydration in a format that any given species can make use of best is critical to the maintenance of the D3 cycle and all of its biological offshoots. Tree-dwellers should have access to vertical running water, ideally through rain systems. The required levels of high humidity for all species need a vast amount of more research. We must start to realise that leaving a bowl of water placed inside of an enclosure cannot provide hydration in the way that many species have evolved to utilise it. We also must factor in ambient humidity and collection via capillary action as pointed out in 'The Arcadia Guide to Reptile and Amphibian Nutrition'. We must view the provision of light, energy from light, diet, hydration, and physical and mental enrichment as a homogenous process that works together for the benefit of the animal, and that every aspect of care, including the light and shade method, works together to make this possible. This therefore can be classed as ethical and effective captive reptile care.

"Cuban Knight Anole drinking during spraying"

The Importance
of PAR

The sun is the driving force, the sustaining energy, behind all life. Without it, we have no life. The sun can and should be viewed as pure energy—a life-giving and sustaining force that surrounds us and helps to nourish us. Whether this 'energy' is taken as direct 'energy' as heat or from the transfer of light to food, and along the vast and intricate food chain, we simply cannot survive without the sun. As such, we should view 'light', in all of its terrestrial wavelengths, as energy. If we can succeed in changing our mind-sets to this type of thinking, we will find it much easier to accept these principles. It is true that a huge percentage of the 'terrestrial' wavelengths of light projected to earth, as yet, remain invisible to humans; this in itself does not mean that they are not there, not potent and effective, and not important. By effective, I mean that every species, whether plant or animal, will have a use for these wavelengths in some form or in some guise.

Light, whether taken directly from the sun or from a reflection from a white stone or from a wet leaf, has an intimate and powerful interaction with all of the life around it. We all know that plants need light; it is, after all, one of the driving forces behind photosynthesis—most of us will have conducted basic experiments in primary school where you place a sticking plaster or piece of masking tape over a leaf and leave it for a week or so. When the tape is removed, the plant has discoloured underneath. This is an easy way to establish just how potent and life-sustaining light is. But plants use light in many amazing ways. They absorb it, they use it through photosynthesis to turn light into sugars, and, of course, they fragment and reflect it. This, in itself, is core to the survival of many hundreds of species of animal of all kinds.

Photosynthesis, of course, is dependent on many parameters; these include a plant having access to light and water, food and air (including CO_2), but light in itself must be provided to the plant in the right quantity (strength, brightness, power) and in the right wavelengths (colours) for the plant to be fully able to make use of the light in photosynthesis and to show continued and sustained growth.

We must refer to natural sunlight as being truly 'full spectrum'. The earth's atmosphere either reflects or absorbs the non-terrestrial wavelengths and stops them from effecting us in a negative way. This protective action simply means that all of the terrestrial (the safe wavelengths that are projected through the atmosphere and are common to earth) wavelengths of light would be projected effectively, and would be available from the far blue to the long wavelength infra-red ends of the spectrum. All of these wavelengths, of course, have to have a use, and plants and animals will have found a use for them. We refer to short wavelength and, as such, invisible blue as being ultra-violet and long red as infra-red—again invisible to humans as heat.

Plants need a light source that offers certain peaks of light, whether such peaks are visible or invisible to humans, to be able to grow properly. We know that both the colour blue and red are vital to the core processes of photosynthesis; this, in itself, has led to a level of industry and of keeper confusion. You may have seen some plant growth LED lamps in reptile or hydroponic shops that have a collection of bright red and blue chips. These have been placed in the mix of lamps with the hope of providing the plant with these core peaks in blue or red. In truth—and as science and tech have developed—this thinking has become very much out-of-date. In actual fact, this thinking is now not only out of date but also recognised as detrimental to enclosure-bound plants and animals as this array of colour can negatively impact on the total colour (CRI) of the enclosure as the human keeper perceives it and a critical reduction in the level of PAR. I will explain why.

As always, we need to look to the sun for our answers. The sun does not have visible shafts or columns of bright red and blue light, or indeed any other one colour; rather, it is a homogenous colour that we refer to as being 'full spectrum'. By this, we mean that every terrestrial wavelength is catered for in a measured and balanced way. Red and blue are indeed essential parts of the mix. We can see these colours, as suggested previously, when sunlight is passed through a prism, for example. We also know all too well how essential terrestrial Ultraviolet is to life and, of course, what would happen to the earth with no heat.

"A single 9w Arcadia Jungle Dawn in use through a small mesh topped vivarium"

We, as keepers, on the other hand, have to use artificial light sources to illuminate and provide energy to our animals. These sources have very real limitations and can never be thought of as 'miniature suns'. Yes, technology is advancing—we have seen huge gains in the forms of High Output T5 UVB projecting lamps, T5 Power compacts and with LED—but these lamps are still far from perfection. Accordingly, we have to factor in these inherent limitations; we have to work with them and adjust our lighting systems and our enclosures so that every given species can go on to obtain the level of energy that it requires. As such, we should not seek to provide our systems with a light source that is split into colour segments; this has a very real limitation in of itself. The problem with both red and blue as wavelengths is that, when used on their own, they have a real lack of energy behind them. By energy, we refer to LUX, Lumens, and, of course, by measuring and quantifying PAR (Photosynthetically active radiation).

Measuring PAR relates to the way we place a value of energy behind the photons of light between 400 and 700 nm. We can term this measurement (PAR) as the effective 'power' or 'quantity' behind any given light source. In real terms, a 6.5k Kelvin LED of 3 watts may have a PAR of 300 when measured at 10 cm from the lamp to the metre; this would enable good levels of growth. A 3watt 460-480nm Blue LED, when measured at the same

"A live planted system"

distance, may only have a PAR of much less than 100. Therefore, we have two light sources of the same driven power but one with a more usable or available energy (PAR) than the other going forward, and would have a greater positive impact with regard to both growth rates, plant health and human colour rendition.

For ideal plant-growth, we should aim for a level of PAR of 100 as an absolute minimum from 10 cm from the light source to the very topmost leaf and for shade dwelling plants. Ideally, this PAR should be much higher (300-700) depending on the species of plant. We should also keep in mind that our enclosures should look clean and display crisp and natural colours, and that they offer a measured gradient from light to shade. We should not over-provide light in terms of quantity, either to a plant or an animal that has no chance of escape. The sun, of course, is very much more powerful than any lamp, but at least a wild animal has the opportunity to run away, bury or hide. Our enclosures should be designed with good thought and with the needs of the species of both plant and animal in mind. The lighting system, including the provision of heat can then be designed around the species to be housed in that particular sized and type enclosure.

A light colour of 6.5k kelvin is generally referred to as being 'full spectrum' or 'natural sunlight'. If we weight a light source with single red and blue light sources—and especially when using LEDs, which are, by definition, a spot source—we do nothing but generate long columns of largely un-usable light over specific areas that is weak in PAR. In effect, we end up with 'disco' stripes. This will also interfere with the total colour of light or 'CRI', and, as a result, the enclosure will end up looking purple instead of a natural crisp warm white, 5.5-7 k kelvin (this range of colour would be acceptable as a homogenous colour to represent natural daylight).

It therefore is better to use a suitable 'full spectrum' light source, whether a reflected linear fluorescent lamp or an LED source that does cater for the whole terrestrial spectrum (5.5k-7k kelvin) and

"22w Arcadia Jungle Dawn LED plant growth lamp"

projects the required level of PAR to the plants that we keep and provides enough visible light for the vertebrate inhabitants.

If we can be sure of maintaining these parameters, there really isn't a species of plant that cannot be kept and grown successfully, and also, with regard to those plants we grow on purpose to fulfil part of the diet, maintaining a correct PAR will help to ensure that the plant is as nutritious as the substrate will allow it to become.

I recently tested a branded LED plant growth lamp that purported to have everything in its make up to allow for plant growth. The mix was a straight-forward mix of white and blue chips, but the chips were so poorly selected and under-driven, where the level of PAR, even 10 cm from the chips, was measuring only 17 on average. This went down, of course, where the LEDs did not converge. There is no way that a system providing a PAR of 17 can sustain plant life long-term; even the shade dwelling mosses would struggle with that. As such, we suggest that a minimum PAR of 100 be provided at the topmost leaf for shade dwelling species and increasing from there in a pertinent fashion.

What about UV? Well, it is often said that plants need UV to grow. In a sense, that is correct but they also have developed a level of

"A growing Bio-Active system for Pygmy Chameleons"

protection against UV. In fact, if we over-provide UV to a plant that equates to a level that it has not yet evolved to utilise, all too quickly it will start to burn (as with every other species on earth, both flora and fauna). You will commonly see brown burns start to appear towards the leaf's tips and edges, and then progress inwards the leaf itself. This is why a single Fluorescent Reptile light source should not be used as a one stop grow lamp, although it could form part of a dedicated and well-designed plant-growth system in both agriculture and in exotic animal care.

The provision of light must be as balanced as in nature. If we use a light source with a low level of PAR, i.e A T8 reptile lamp but with a high percentage of UVB, the plant will indeed suffer. The PAR that is available from this type of light source will not allow good cell regeneration quick enough, whilst all the time the UV continues to cause damage. In actual fact, we need to have a balanced ratio of PAR alongside UV so that the plant repairs and continues to grow, regardless of any adverse effects of UV in an enclosed space.

For us, as forward-thinking reptile keepers, we understand the vast importance of UV in its two terrestrial wavelength groups. We use it already and are well-versed in the outcomes of not doing so. If we match the needs of the plants to the needs of our animals, and if we use full-spectrum UV sources alongside

> It is also worth pointing out that plants must have access to total darkness, just as is required by reptiles, to complete the cycles required to flourish."

our dedicated plant-growth systems, they not only will help to sustain plant growth but also to achieve our goals of Wild Re-Creation™ and ethical, Bio-Active keeping.

It is also worth pointing out that plants must have access to total darkness, just as is required by reptiles, to complete the cycles required to flourish. The principles of extending and reducing illuminated periods for different cycles or life stages of a plant are well-documented in plant care science. For those systems where large crops are required quickly, an illuminated period of 16 or 18 hours a day is used to force a plants to grow quickly. The lighting period then is reduced to induce flowering and, as such, speed-up the yield of crop. As can be seen, even in agriculture, darkness still forms part of the growth cycle, as it should. In short, leaving the lights of the viv in for unnaturally long periods will not cause your plants to bed-in quickly or grow quickly to fill, quite the reverse. Good, stable growth can take time, but you will be left with fit, healthy plants that will flourish for long periods of time, and that will flower and fill the animal's living space as you have need.

Bio-Activity and its Place in the Hobby

I recently was asked if I felt that there really was a long-term place in the modern-day keeping of exotics for the theory of Bio-Activity. Was this move really all that important in the grand scheme of things or could it be that this worldwide C change in practise was simply a push by well-known brands into gaining further sales or simply the advent of yet another 'fad' or 'fashion'? I must admit to feeling quite horrified and altogether disappointed that someone could still actually question the uses and critical interactions of the thinking behind Bio-Active systems, but it got me thinking as we must continually do so: 'What do I really believe and why and can that be backed up with both science and history?'

I, myself, have a firm, unswaying belief that it is with the accurate and measured Wild Re-Creation™ of a captive system per species in which all of the answers to all of our keeping questions are held. I firmly believe that it is with the proper implementation of this theory that we will see captive exotics truly thrive in each and every way. But, exotic pets have been kept for the past few decades on a mix of what I would now term as largely inappropriate and sometimes quite dangerous manmade substrates—good old newspaper, underpowered lighting and heating systems, poor or ill-informed mineral and vitamin provision, poor hydration and dietary shortfalls due to lack of choice and availability. In this time, it is true to say, nevertheless, that we have witnessed an explosion of positive captive breeding results. Certainly, quite common species of animal now continue to go on to appear to do very well indeed. Look at the crested gecko, cornsnake and royal/ball python for great examples of population explosion. So, is a Wild Re-Created system and the associated mind-set really required or can we revert back to course gravels, newspaper, nasty coir, underpowered lighting and ill-fitted heating, poor hydration and mineral provision and one-species diets?

Firstly, we must remember that, before commercial reptile products became available, most pet reptiles were kept in a basic form of bio-activity in as much as many keepers used gathered soils or local sands. Some added pot plants and, of course, some used paper. It is only quite recently, really, that sands and woodchips and the like have become available en-masse and branded towards the hobby. In truth, we now can see that it was, with these good intentions, that many of the avoidable problems started.

We also must remember that many reptile keepers used to collect their own foods from the locality around them in terms of plants and insects, and used to breed their own rodents. These insect diets were supplemented with farmed mealworms and then crickets and locusts, but again, it is only fairly recently in the whole grand scheme of things that we, as a group of keepers, have had access to mass-produced feeders with some, I feel, now quite deficient of full-spectrum nutrition. As such, the 'grandfathers' of our hobby were offering a vast variety of insects, actually pretty much anything that their nets could capture, all of which were feeding on wild plants, exposed to natural sunlight and were up to temperature and full of natural sugars and so on. They also were breeding feeder rodents in small batches, all the time knowing what they had been fed on and kept in.

So, back in history, keepers used natural substrates and collected local feeds, but again many animals still did not do well long-term. Those keepers in hotter climates did better, of course, as they had access to outside enclosures and therefore all of the energy available outside. We must, as such, make a distinction between the successes of breeders in the hotter climates and those of us that struggled through in northern European, for instance, with very little access to natural, unfiltered heat and light for extended periods. (I remember, in the late-1980s, having an adult male and wild collected waterdragon dropped off in our shop as unwanted. The almost lifeless lizard was in a very sorry state, being kept in a glass-fronted tea chest with nothing but a blue-dipped tungsten 'daylight' lamp for energy. It was an early spring day in the UK with temperatures of no more than 16 degrees. I took the dragon outside and laid it on top of a car in the spring sunlight. I stayed with the lizard with one hand hovering over its back for around a quarter of an hour until it started to raise its head and move around. I then restrained the animal and faced it directly into the sun for as long as I could manage it (I was quite young at the time!). The animal recovered and fed not long after before going off to a better enclosure. These were the days before mass UV and heat systems—the bad old days of black lights—but even this low amount of solar energy on a chilly spring day in the UK was enough to bring the poor thing round. I learned a lesson that day, and it is one that I have taken into my professional life: nature is pre-programmed to survive, and will do so if it has access to the parameters it has evolved to use.)

We then were able to provide heat in a kind of a controlled fashion. At first, quite dangerously, with an upturned lightbulb seated inside of a terracotta pot or an aquarium heater placed in a milk bottle full of water. (Both of these methods offer inappropriate heat and are very dangerous indeed to both animal and keeper,

"A young Water Dragon"

but this was the start of the large advancements in technology.) Then, with the introduction of brewer's heat pads and then heat mats and spot lamps, we shot forward with heating choices. As you can see by the proliferation of specified product now, we started to see controlled heat as being vitally important—and, of course, it is and always will be.

Then, we saw the many and harrowing issues regarding demineralisation; two and two were put together, and branded calcium powders became available, and soon after, full-spectrum vitamin concoctions were introduced and then became the norm. As such our animals started to do that little bit better as the synthetics allowed more biological function. Then, of course, the UVB lamp arrived in concept, which started a vast change in the hobby and, further, bit by bit, helped to increase success rates and lowered the number of cases of debilitating and now quite avoidable MBD in all of its murderous forms. The first lamps used were mainly black lights, which look terrible and are heavily weighted towards UVA, offering only around half of one percent UVB. Having said that, however, animals moved their positions and got very close to these lamps and, in some small way, did that little bit better. This tech continued and, in this day, continues to improve and to adapt as we seek to Re-Create average wild UV indexes and to match those power gradients with good heat provision, foods, and the all-important effective provision of thorough hydration. Even with all of these fantastic advances, however, we still witness ghastly amounts of impaction and MBD, poor shedding, and some species that should be easy to breed simply not reproducing or reproducing but babies not surviving. (See the Mellor's chameleon as an example of this type of situation. The good news is that, with the addition of much improved and, as such, Wild Re-Created systems, the adults now can be tempted not only to carry on breathing but also to willingly reproduce. The eggs are, on the whole, fertile, and many hatch. It then is in the first few months that some of the young tend to expire. This may be due to a lack of an external source of energy, a lack of adequate hydration or a critical part of the adapted diet being found missing or lacking. If we can ascertain this shortfall and plug the gap, the young should all survive and the species become readily available as captive-bred ex-situ.)

We can, of course, surmise that impaction can be quite easily quantified and eradicated with safer, more natural particulate substrates, better hydration and, of course, the proper provision of heat from the right wavelengths. We also can quite honestly state that the fact that MBD is even still seen in collections today simply means that we still have much to learn and still have much to change. We also can see how inappropriate humidity and a poor

> We should seek to—and must never stop—learning, changing, and adapting our systems so that they really do start to provide for the core and evolved biological needs of the many differing species that we keep."

diet can negatively affect shedding and that all of these things can be fixed through Bio-Activity through Wild Re-Creation™.

We should seek to—and must never stop—learning, changing, and adapting our systems so that they really do start to provide for the core and evolved biological needs of the many differing species that we keep. The recent boom of interest in the Bio-Active and Wild Re-Created systems, in a sense, is a step back in time (with a difference); of course, however, we must also accept that, in order to truly move forward, we must also look to the past. We can easily change and adapt our history, taking and implementing the good and leaving the ineffective as a distant if not humorous memory. The latest incarnation of Bio-Activity really does represent the very best of the worldwide-gathered knowledge to which we now have access. Couple this together with very quickly advancing technology and we really do start to drill down into effective species' care and accordingly lay the foundations for the next decade of continued vast improvement.

Is there a place in the hobby for Bio-Active systems? Well, the answer, yet again, is an emphatic yes. It hasn't actually really left us at all! It is just that mass-produced—and, with hindsight, poorly designed products—became easier to obtain and were much more affordable. Word of the inclusion of these mass-produced products spread, and these now quite ineffective systems, I feel, sadly became the norm.

Bio-Activity through Wild Re-Creation™ really does offer the best of all worlds. It is nicer for the keeper to view, better for the animal, and much less work in terms of in viv maintenance. It greatly reduces the emerging risks of VOC-release from petrochemicals and allows the system to feed the system in a myriad of important and complex ways. Animals can hide; they can obtain hydration in the best possible way and can live a full and reproductively successful life in a largely stress-free environment. In short, we can conclude that, if the simple rules are followed, we will indeed see much less incidence of disease and other problems, better reproduction, and positive genetic pass-on, and we will see science back this up day-by-day through better research and the continued development of new products that will allow us all, as keepers, to continue to improve.

"A basking Mountain Horned Dragon, *A Capra*"

As keepers, of course, we must intervene, as is our duty, and as required. We need to feed our animals and monitor water levels, make good substrate and plant choices, continue our health checks and maintain our heat and light systems. We also should have our animals screened for unhelpful parasites on a regular basis. This is now very simple and should form part of ongoing good husbandry for all keepers. We must also factor in, as a point of importance, the interaction between the enclosure and its inhabitants. We must think of it all at the macro level first. We must accept the millions of variations of power gradients that are available with the light and shade method and all of their infinite uses. We must factor in the critical work that the enclosure custodians, including springtails, perform, and their own transference of nutrition into the diets of our pets. Moreover, we must accept that consuming one's habitat is a natural process that should be free from risk and can remain very positive at all times. We must keep in mind the proliferation of soil-bound positive bacteria and other microscopic life, and its own positive effect on gut flora. Further, we must always and continually look for the next new development, the latest science, and the latest positive report of captive breeding.

So does effective and ethical 'Bio-Activity' through 'Wild Re-Creation™' have a place in our hobby? In my mind, the question should be 'Can we still think of our hobby as being both effective and ethical without 'Bio-Activity' through 'Wild Re-Creation™'?'

Pre-Biotics and Pro-Biotics

A nimals, like all other life forms, including our own species— and, of course, the entire eco-system in which the subject dwells right from the macro to the giant (this is where we, as forward-thinking keepers, must focus)—are the hosts to and have an interaction with a myriad of complex micro-organism systems, all of which exist within and around the body. Each and every single one of these sometimes quite basic lifeforms will have some kind of function and/or interaction with another neighbouring organism at some level, whether that be critical or incidental. In most situations, these interactions are wholly beneficial, if not a vital biological requirement within or around the animals that live in such an ecosystem. Think of the changes and adaptations that your own immune system makes every second of your life, awake or asleep, with the sole aim of protecting you from infection and disease, and allowing you to continue to grow and develop through all of the natural stages of life. The same processes are true for the rest of biology, without exception.

We can take this kind of deep, quite serious thinking right down to a genomic level, of course, and I am sure that science will continue to change and adapt so as to allow us to do so very accurately in good time. The constant interaction between the environment, as a whole, and genetic variance is an ever further growing field of research which will, in time, start to show us not only the vitally important health and wellbeing factors in the human species, but also in the wider groups of the earth's animals as this research progresses and becomes more usable and better understood over the years. We then could start to factor in targeted drug therapy for accurately diagnosed disease. We may also be able to make enclosure and environmental changes so as to ensure a natural level of disease limitation in some susceptible animals.

As this technology progresses, we will, of course, see real benefits from the prescription of personalised medications per patient in, once again, both the human and the animal. This will not only be effective, but further could reduce both treatment times and costs whilst offering a welcome increase in positive therapeutic effect and disease modification, and a potential reduction in the number, or severity, of unwelcome side effects. We actually ae not too far away from this important and very exciting move forward in human medicine, which will, of course, then filter along

An out-of-balance microorganism load or one that is, in its own nature, 'hostile' can cause disease in and of itself."

into the hands of suitable vets and, eventually, into the animals for which we care so much.

There is, as you will expect, an increasing appreciation that this plethora of organisms is not only important to the maintenance of long-term positive health and wellbeing, but also, and reversely, to the manifestation of disease, both infectious and non-infectious. An out-of-balance microorganism load or one that is, in its own nature, 'hostile' can cause disease in and of itself. As such, our own research and development with regard to the exact care of exotic animals will start to show up more and more of the potent interactions between a full and varied, well though-out diet, high levels of positive gut flora, enrichment at all levels, and the ever widening and intricate interaction between the enclosure and its inhabitants.

We are all, by now, quite well aware of the many published benefits of so called pro-biotics and increasing the numbers of positive gut flora (bacteria) within the human biome. It is thought that, if the levels of useful alimentary canal-dwelling bacteria (from mouth to vent) are large enough in quantity and quality and are living in good enough health themselves, that the patient (man or animal) then would be able to utilise this bacterial symbiosis not only to fight off infection in a more robust fashion but also, as I believe, to assimilate and to use more of the individual elements of the foods that have been consumed. Some may say that these microorganisms are indeed the fuel to the fire of increasing health and well-being. There is, however, and always will be, a counter argument to the reverse.

With regard to any of these purported limitations, we must exercise caution as we would with any and all new inclusion. Act on the advice of a vet if at all unsure, and steer towards the little and often approach. Those animals that have diagnosed kidney issues, any of the metabolic diseases or have had a long period of infection, may need closely monitoring.

To re-cap:

A Pro-Biotic is a culture of live, safe bacteria, usually in powdered form or as a suspension. They are commonly sold for human use in yogurts, powders or as compressed tablets. These bacteria are usually labelled as being 'good' or 'beneficial'. There are many strains of thought with regard to their use and efficacy in both humans and animals, but behind the 'scientific babble' there is a very good and quite understandable theory. Many sources proclaim that these bacteria are a gateway towards a new age of health and wellbeing, and that they will help to colonise the gut and go on to allow the gut to perform as it should—or has done in the past history of man. Other sources deny any useful interaction or effect at all. There must therefore be some kind of workable middle ground where both benefits and limitations can be assessed and quantified, and the uses and limitations made sense of and utilised in an effective fashion. In real terms, however, a probiotic culture, however effective, can only really be truly effective if it has a 'food' source. We call this 'food' a 'Pre-Biotic'. In reality, a pre-biotic is, on the whole, a source of dietary fibre. Both pea and beets are the most commonly used Pre-Biotics.

Pro-Biotics are, I feel, designed to make up for yet another set of dietary shortfalls. Once again, look to the evolution and adaptation of the human animal: it is only quite recently that we have started to meticulously wash and to sterilise everything, including ourselves and our foods. As such, we have forgone 'wild' access to certain good and, of course, reversely bad bacterial cultures, and also soil-dwelling vitamins and minerals. I myself recently undertook a course and, as part of the syllabus, saw a brief video lecture of a 'microbiome' experiment being conducted with a rural tribe in Tanzania by the University of Colorado Boulder. This video demonstrated, through film and with the use of published results of the laboratory testing of collected cultures, that these very rural peoples that largely still lead a hunter-gatherer lifestyle, did not suffer many of the diseases to which humanity has become so susceptible. It also showed that this tribe had vastly greater levels or numbers of useful gut flora, and that a Western visitor, if integrated into the community and after undertaking their own eating and drinking practices, would, over time, also see a marked increase in the numbers of useful gut-dwelling bacteria in all sections of the gut.

This research was more than illuminating for me as I started to see a correlation between the low rates of common disease and increased levels of health in these humans. I wondered very quickly whether the reverse could be said for reptiles when removed from the beneficial systems of the wild. It is also worth pointing out that rates of Vitamin B deficiency in the human are reported to be at an all-time high, leading to a significant growth, once again, in vitamin compound sales. I also believe this to be true for the captive reptile. Again, please do not misunderstand me: I am not for once second suggesting that you rush out and eat anything and everything right from the 'mud' of the city garden in an unwashed state. Indeed, our own systems may not cope with

"Eyed Lizards"

the potential extra load leading to all sorts of nasty issues, but I do hope that you can start to see that we now have a reduced eco-system interaction. As a result, we, as a species, are having to add back into our diets the bacteria that is required to help us fight infection and to carry on living in a healthy or productive way. The same indeed can be surmised, I feel, when considering the captive care of exotic animals of all kinds.

If an animal has been denied access to the wild, it will not have access to the wild cultures that sustain it in its developed wild state. Our reinvented system of Wild Re-Creation™ through Bio-Activity surely will help to make up some of the historical shortfall, if maintained correctly, but the animal still may need 'topping up' in much the same way as we 'top-up' the missing vitamins and minerals in their diet with powders. As such, we soon will arrive at a time in the hobby where Pro-Biotics are offered for use with or in reptile foods. These cultures must be used alongside a Pre-Biotic source of fibre and, as such, I suggest that you conduct further reading into the topic and analyse the food sources that you use to make sure that this interaction is catered for effectively.

It could simply be that a low dose of a mix of Pro-Biotic agents, when fed alongside a good Pre-Biotic as part of the usual feed, is indeed beneficial, and that it will help an animal to fight potential infection, shed effectively, and go on to reproduce without issue. Its inclusion could be another aid in our constant quest for ethical reptile care through Wild Re-Creation™. It also could be that they are used in higher doses under the prescriptive advice of a vet in times of illness or indeed after travel or reproduction. It is indeed early days, but I must say that I feel that these changes and advances are very positive.

Manuka Honey and Bee Pollen

M anuka honey is another one of life's so called 'super-foods', sold to the masses as a cure-all. We all will have seen this product in the supermarkets and health food shops and, for some, it does seem to have an almost miraculous therapeutic effect. There also is quite good chemical analysis on the product, which does, in some way, back-up a number of the claims. Honey, after all, is considered a natural product, included in the diets of most if not all early humans.

Manuka honey is made by bees native to New Zealand. These bees collect pollen solely from the Manuka bush (*Leptospermum scoparium*). This plant is well known as having powerful anti-bacterial benefits; this does appear to be passed on to the bees and remains as active within the honey. There are, as one might expect, many uses for Manuka honey in modern herpetoculture, both as a food and as a salve. The question, of course, pertains to how many species of reptile seek out pure wild honey and whether there is an evolved requirement for it?

In short, I guess it is very difficult to know for sure: the tree monitors would be keen, of this I am very sure! Most reptiles are true omnivores and, as such, will consume anything that they possibly can as quickly as they can. Our knowledge of wild feeding is increasing very quickly now, but the sheer amount of data needed to ascertain exactly what every species consumes will surely take a long period of time. We also are now able to see very quickly via the written word, social media and via film, evidence of certain species eating items that we once never thought possible. (I recently saw a corn snake eating an egg on film. I have had a hunch for many years that they would indeed do so as part of an opportunistic diet made up from rodents, birds, reptiles, amphibians, inverts and pretty much anything else that they can fit in their mouths, but had never seen proof until 2015.) Further, of course, these animals may benefit from consuming a prey source that itself has consumed wild honey and therefore it would be made available via the usual transfer of the contents of the alimentary system.

In truth, it is far too ambiguous to say for sure one way or the other; however, we can see a definite list of positives for its safe and measured inclusion into the hobby. We can see a therapeutic effect, both when provided for in the diet and when used as a natural topical salve with an aim of aiding healing and reducing

> Manuka honey could be a useful addition into the medicine box of the modern-day reptile-keeper as it has many positives and very few negatives."

the risk of infection. We can see that, when used in moderation and as part of a full and varied diet, there are very few negatives other than a sudden boost of sugars. As such, we should view this largely certified organic product as a 'supplement' rather than as a food to be used when required, and in moderation.

There is good evidence for its use in skin-healing in reptiles after injury or surgery. It also is very good for the speedy healing of burns. The honey itself is used after cleaning of the wound to act as an antiseptic and to speed-up the general healing process. Likewise, there is the wild occurrence of animals seeking out the honey after injury and self-medicating in New Zealand.

Manuka honey could be a useful addition into the medicine box of the modern-day reptile-keeper as it has many positives and very few negatives. However, it is on the vastly different product 'Bee Pollen' that I would like to concentrate now.

Bee Pollen

Bee pollen is yet another one of those so-called super-foods; in this case, I am more likely to agree with the statement. Bee Pollen is actually the natural and collected pollen balls from the legs of the worker bees. It is the result of the usual daily pollen collection and is used inside of the hive as a food when mixed with propolis and bee saliva for both the queen and the bee larvae. Bee Pollen has been used in human medicine, beauty products and foods for thousands of years. It is an entirely natural product that, as part of its make up, has a plethora of natural and very bio-available, proteins, amino acids, full-spectrum vitamins and minerals. In fact, it has been given to very sick or older people with reduced appetite as it is believed to stimulate feeding and has a useful amount of protein—some research suggesting as much as 40%. Historically, it has been collected quite naturally as a percentage of it falls from the hive. More recently—and for commercial purposes—collection has been carried out via methods that safely remove a percentage of the pollen from the bee as it enters the hive. Beekeepers have to be very careful not to over-harvest or the colony will not be able to replicate and thrive.

Bee Pollen is reported to be packed full of the broad spectrum of vitamins and minerals. It is a very good source of broad-spectrum and bio-available B group vitamins in particular. It is also a very

"Bee Pollen"

powerful source of amino acids and, of course, useful and readily available sugars.

In terms of Wild Re-Creation™, it is more likely that a wild reptile would encounter Bee Pollen than it would pure wild honey. Pollen, in and of itself, is a useful addition to the diet and, of course, makes up a natural part of the diet of many of those species that eat flowers and/or the insects that gather around them. In my mind, the vast benefits of Bee Pollen strongly point towards its safe and measured inclusion into the modern diets of captive animals.

> Bee Pollen has been shown to aid wound-healing and help fight infection, improve appetite, lower the rate of inflammation and, of course, be useful with the provision of full-spectrum sugars, Amino acids, vitamins and minerals."

For a long time now, I have been bothered by the interaction of certain reptiles and flowers/pollen, and the fact that it has been difficult if not impossible to safely recreate this wild interaction in captivity. We all know that certain geckos, especially those referred to as Day Geckos (phelsuma, lygodactylus sp, etc.), will readily lick pollen from flowers just as they consume the sugary secretions of aphids. The larger species, including iguanas, will seek out pollen-rich flowers, including those huge and pollen-dense Hibiscus blooms. They have adapted to doing so; therefore, there must be a reason and a use behind so doing. Could it be that the addition of pollen in the form of these collected globules of Bee Pollen is yet another one of these missing links in the captive diet? I currently think so, yes—one of many.

Bee Pollen has been shown to aid wound-healing and help fight infection, improve appetite, lower the rate of inflammation and, of course, be useful with the provision of full-spectrum sugars, Amino acids, vitamins and minerals. The list of benefits are almost endless, including an increased level of blood oxygenation which, in and of itself, could help to further limit those knock-on nutritional imbalances and accordingly improve other biological functions, including the natural D3 cycle. Therefore, there are many of positives—but are there any negatives? At the point of writing, I can see none if the food is used sensibly. I do, however, offer a word of caution for those that are sensitive to bee or wasp stings and those with formal allergies: it would be advisable to refrain from direct interaction.

Again, a 'little and often approach' may be useful as is its inclusion into gut-loading formulae. I also have seen positive results with the inclusion of Bee Pollen into the diets of both chelonia (as a group) and *Iguana iguana.* In both cases, the product was readily consumed and activity levels increased. Again, there are many reports of its use and interactions online. Some claim that it is a cure-all for reptiles and as powerful as some prescribed antibiotics in terms of infection control its ability to literally clean out the gut and leave only good bacteria in its wake or that it will act like some kind of mythical reptilian viagra. Much of this is likely to be proverbial 'snake oil', but behind every madness is a certain dose of sensibility. Any increase in blood oxygenation would be helpful, that much is certain.

Bee Pollen may indeed be the perfect pick-me-up for sick or recuperating animals. It may provide a sudden boost of energy and B vitamins that spur-on an episode of reproduction. It may be a useful source of food to be used to replicate some of the missing levels of wild pollen in the diet of herbivores and omnivores; it also may well have some sort of useful anti-bacterial effect. For me, any single one of these is the least important reason to include it into the diet. We, as forward-thinking keepers, have to think holistically, about the whole animal and in all of its life stages and environmental interactions. We have to attempt to see the bigger picture. If an animal has changed and adapted to require a certain level of broad spectrum nutrition from many food sources in the wild, then we must seek to provide these 'many' food sources in captivity or we may just miss out an essential ingredient that will allow the subject to thrive.

There certainly are plenty of observations of lizards from the groups Agamid, Lacertid, Varanus and gecko actively predating upon flowers. This food source is not simply only applicable to Phelsuma and Lygodactylus species, nor it is just for Iguanids, Chelonia or the even the bearded dragon. It seems that flowers provide a welcome source of energy from sugars and protein for wild reptiles. Of course, they also help the plant in return via pollination, by scattering seeds from consumed fruits via faecal matter and, of course, with predatory insect control.

"A fine example of the Fiji Iguana"

Using Bee Pollen in a safe and measured way, either as a whole source as part of a full and varied diet, or as part of a vitamin-based dietary supplement or indeed through the gut-loading of live feeders will simply help to narrow the gap between historical wild provision, and that of the historical under provision of the captive animal. If an animal has developed so as to obtain full-spectrum nutrition through a vast and complex feeding regime, then it will require the same kind of processes and foods to be able to go on to thrive in captivity. There is, as we now know, no individual commercial powder that will magically do it all for

"Rhinoceros Iguana"

us; no single food source or feeding plan that is fool-proof and will supply every single item of nutrition that your exact animal will ever need. No, we have to constantly think about the 'full-spectrum' of dietary provision right down to the minerals and microbes that live in soil that then interact with the plants that feed the insects that feed the reptiles and so on and so forth. Pollen, on the whole, I feel, is an essential item missing from the diets of many captive exotics. As such, Bee Pollen can be used to help to make up for this shortfall. Bee Pollen is stated as being non-toxic and cannot yet be synthesised or overdosed.

Bee Pollen contains (including but not exhaustive): Arginine, Histidine, Isoleucine, Leucine, Lysine, Methionine, Phenylalanine, Threonine, Trypophan, Valine, Potassium, Magnesium, Calcium, Copper, Iron, Silicon, Phosphorous, Sulphur, Chlorine, Manganese, B vitamins (Thiamine, Riboflavin, Nicotinic acid, pyridoxine, panthothenic acid, Biotin, Folic acid), Lactoflavine, Alpha/Beta Carotene, vitamin C, vitamin D, Flavoxanthine, Xanthophyll, Flavonols, Lycopene, water, sugars.

Plants and Mosses

One thing that will always firmly tie the world's Bio-Active system keepers to one another is, of course, the inclusion of live plants into the systems they create and maintain. As forward-thinking keepers, for many years we have tried to keep plants alive inside of our enclosures but, on the whole, this has not been historically successful; just look at how many plastic and silk plants are now available to reptile-keepers—the range is amazing, even if the chemical composition, botanical detail and finish is not. They were all developed for a good reason, and that reason was to ensure that fellow keepers could provide some kind of greenery and decoration inside of a harsh and very unforgiving system.

The good news is that we now have moved on from these largely 'bad old days' of fakery and 'making do'. Technology has changed and it has adapted, meaning we now can maintain effective care systems 'for life' that not only allow live plants to grow but will allow them, like our animals, to thrive for years to come. This is a new era in reptile, amphibian and invert care; a revolution of positive and exacting provision through good science and ever-improving technology. All we have to do, as keepers, is embrace the changes in a pertinent fashion and implement the right changes per species into our systems in a 'Safe' and 'Measured' way.

The process of live planting and the allocation of plants per species or group is a huge subject, of course. There are literally hundreds of species of plant available over much of the year for us to use, learn from and enjoy. These plants now can be found in reptile stores, online, in supermarkets and, of course, in local horticultural centres. There is an amazing array of species from all continents and in all colours, shapes and sizes. As such, there really is a plant or several plants that can be found easily for every size and type of enclosure. There is both beauty and function to be found in plants, from the macro mosses and alpines right up giant rubber and banana plants. Each will have a use and each can be placed to perform a job at certain locations within an enclosure. Vivarium and terrarium decoration is no longer a question of how many plastic skulls and plastic cacti to place inside, but is a well thought-out process of function, interaction and lasting design.

The thoughtful inclusion of live plants can turn a good enclosure into a truly great one. Please remember that live plants do not act only as an attractive distraction for a keeper but also allow an animal to find natural shade and security. They will disperse light and energy from light, and they will help to maintain positive air quality and stabilise humidity. They therefore can be thought of as part of the provision of core positive enrichment. In my own mind, I am sure that we are yet to even scratch the surface with regards to just how positive a force that live plants can be for captive exotics.

Before I carry on any further, I will point out one obvious thing: the plants that are available to us, on the whole, are not found in the native environments of the species we keep. Most Bio-Active keepers have had to bite the bullet, as it were, and accept that, in order to maintain a fully functioning system that is live-planted, we will have to use plants that are only not native to the localities of the species of animal that is being kept but that many will have arrived from differing continents also. The hobby itself is split right down the middle in thinking with regards to this frustrating problem: some keepers will spend time seeking out and eventually paying high prices for specific plant species that are only found in the localities of the species they keep, with some keepers obtaining seeds from these nations or specific locations, propagating the said seed and including the exact local plants for that species over a long period of time; other keepers, on the other hand, are happy to use an array of plant species from all over the globe as long as they are safe, attractive and able to 'do the job' that is required of them. In truth, and until the hobby evolves and develops even further as is needed to provide species-specific planting, then both systems have equal value and use. I myself would rather see species- or locality-specific planting, but I realise that, due to the current limitations of price and availability, that that in and of itself is just not possible for many of us. As such, I personally maintain systems that have a variety of plants from differing countries. I have not encountered any issues (other than spontaneous ant colonies appearing), and it is very true to say that the animals do not seem to mind either way.

Plants play a pivotal role in the ongoing and consistent maintenance of the true Bio-Active system; they help to provide and maintain oxygen levels, lower the chances of CO_2 build-ups and regulate the levels of humidity for all types of system, jungle, savannah and arid. They also help to lower the risk of water stagnation. They help to feed the system, but also take nutrients and pass these up the food web. They help to scatter light in a natural way (leaf scatter) and can act very much as an early warning system should anything befall the system. If your plants start to die off for no good reason, take note and take action quickly.

Plants are live entities in their own right. They can and do suffer with genetic problems and/or disease. They can be very hardy or suddenly expire for no good reason. As such, if one plant dies for no apparent reason, it is probably just one of those things. If multiple plants start to wilt and die or a plant that is placed in a certain location seems to suffer on a continuous basis, then you will need to look at your system as a whole and/or in that location, risk of predation and disease, light and food levels. In most cases, slight adjustments to the tech or even making changes to the plant species will fix the issue. The live-planted enclosure keeper will very soon become as knowledgeable about plants and their care as they are about the chosen species of exotic animal.

"Ferns play a vital role in providing light and shade"

> Plants will require some level of maintenance, of course, including thoughtful pruning. They need the right levels of light to thrive (see PAR, wavelengths and quantity), and the correct levels of hydration and humidity per species.

Real plants look wonderful and have numerous benefits to the modern system as a whole. They pose no risk of VOC release when heated, and soon will grow and maybe even flower. They will require some level of maintenance, of course, including thoughtful pruning. They need the right levels of light to thrive (see PAR, wavelengths and quantity), and the correct levels of hydration and humidity per species. They require a source of food—the principle functionality of the Bio-Active system goes a long way to supply this as part of its cyclical process (see feeding your plants alongside your animals later on in this book)—and they also need good airflow (gaseous exchange). If we can provide for all of these in a safe and realistic way, there then is no real reason why any species could not be grown well.

With so many species of plant being so readily available to us, we have to ask ourselves a few basic questions: Which plant species will provide the function that you require best for your animal species? Which plant species are safe for our animals? And what species of plant is most suitable to the rather confined and hot systems we maintain? Which species will flower if that is on your 'must have' list and what kind of environment do they require? Will they need lower light levels or need the full power of the sun to beat down on them all day in order to thrive? These are all basic questions but nonetheless ones that deserve a few moments of thought before rushing into a local plant supplier and spending any money. If you can answer these questions beforehand and even come up with a list of plant species that will cater for the function you require, you will be able to adjust your system to cater to those particular needs. This will ensure that you have done everything possible to cater for the needs of that selection of plants, meaning the chances of plant death reduces, thus saving you extra work and money in the long-run. It is always best to know where you are going before you start.

Firstly, we must pick a range of species of plant that will thrive in all sectors of the vivarium. This is referred to as sensible or 'planned' planting. We then can place high light requirement species closer to a grow lamp or lamps and tuck the shade dwellers further away. We need to replicate the kind of habitat in which the species of plant is most commonly found: for example, if setting up a live planted system for a Leopard Gecko, one would use an organic scrubland or arid mix of soil and volcanic rock. Rocks and dried branches should then be placed inside of the enclosure to provide access to climbing and areas of shelter for self-regulation (enrichment). Arid grasses and members of the Aloe, Harworthia and Crassula family also can be added. The substrate can be maintained at the suitable level of humidity and high levels of light added. Some of the species of springtail that fare well in hotter, drier environments can be added to the enclosure, and the system will, over time and if maintained well, become 'live'. Care must be taken to dissuade live-foods from eating too much of the plants via selective feeding and removal, but other than that, it should all fare quite well. In this type of system, you will also notice that the custodians will dig downwards to a deeper level into the substrate where the humidity percentage is or should be much higher. To check your springtail numbers, you will need to take a sample from the middle to bottom of the substrate. In wet forest systems, the springtails tend to be visible right through the substrate at all levels.

If you wanted to start a system for a pygmy chameleon, carpet moss could be grown on the top of the substrate and indeed over the rocks and up over the cork backgrounds. Bromeliads and tillandsia can be secured with aquatic silicone sealant or wires around the anchor roots and fixed onto rocks, branches and backgrounds. These plants can make for a stunning splash of colour, and indeed will provide a useful function with regards to providing areas of pooled water, shelter and shade, and further will help to maintain important leaf scatter illumination. Pothos or Wandering Jew are both fast-growing climbers that can be grown in almost all systems. They can then be trained from the substrate and grown upwards into the enclosure canopy, intertwining like vines with the more decorative plants. Pothos is a particularly good choice as it grows fast and has long spaces between the 'vine' and the rather heart-shaped, green leaves. This makes this plant a perfect choice for the smaller chameleons to walk along and to find regular hunting and basking points. It is also very hardy, can be cut at will and replanted in soil or water, where it will project new roots and carry on as a new plant. Terrestrial orchids also could be added to provide colour through flower although they need a higher level of maintenance. Ferns and Ficus also are usually added to increase the amount of coverage and visible green; they also can help greatly with humidity maintenance. All of these plants should grow very well indeed, providing their care needs are met. They then can be trained through cutting and wire-fixing along and around the branches and dried vines provided.

"Cushion and Carpet Moss"

Many keepers continue to use potted plants inside of the enclosure. Placing the pot on paper or tiles on the enclosure floor as bare or then covering the pots with substrate to hide them are the usual options; this is usually so that the pots can be lifted out easily for cleaning or moving. In a sense, this method is far better than having no live plants at all, but it does rather defeat the object of total Wild Re-Creation™ through Bio-Activity. Having said that, however, every keeper must be confident with what they are doing and, of course, it is possible that, at times, animals may become sick and need an extra level of care through more sterile surroundings. As such, this method of still maintaining live plants but inside of pots could be quite useful; it is also a useful stepping stone from sterility and plastics towards Bio-Activity and live planting. Care will need to be taken, however: female animals may still lay eggs in the soil, live-food bury into it, and the plants also may become pot-bound. Take care to check the pots when repotting and feeding/watering.

It is also a good idea to remove any soil from the roots of any newly acquired plant. This reduces the risk of pathogen pass-on and allows you to be sure that you are not including any growing hormones used in the horticultural, houseplant trade into your largely organic system. It also reduces the chances of in-situ pest species propagation. I have had many almost magical occurrences of ants and slugs appearing in my larger systems a few weeks after placing in new plants. In most cases, the predator picks them off quite quickly; in other cases, the ants may be toxic and/ or cause harm to the plants, the animals and, of course, any in-situ deposited eggs. Slugs are almost never eaten and almost always become established quickly, consuming plants as they grow.

As such, I suggest that all newly acquired plants are removed from their pots, the soil shaken free into a separate location, and the roots washed and soaked for a short time before being planted into your live system. This only takes a few minutes but can save a lot of work in the long-run.

Moss:

Live moss is another vast asset to the Bio-Active system-keeper, and indeed for the system itself. It is, for most of us with forest and jungle systems, the true 'holy grail' of horticultural triumph. Not only does moss increase the levels of visible green colouration inside of the enclosure, which is pleasant for the keeper, but it also acts as a substrate blanket and a sponge. Moss of the correct, useful species will soak up and retain water, help to control levels of humidity, and will provide a source of welcome cover for custodians and animals alike, whether they are adults, young, or even freshly laid eggs. Moss can be grown all over the vivarium floor and up over fern or coca fibre wall panels. Some species of moss, in time, will grow up over natural rocks and up along branches. It is, on the whole, fairly hardy when settled and with the right care and surroundings can grow quite fast.

There are some rules, of course. The moss that I myself use seems to do best under quite strong full-spectrum lighting with a very high PAR at source. It does not seem to like a super-rich Substrate or constant feeding. Some species seem to prefer to climb upwards towards the light; as such, lamp position can be important. It does, however, require regular and direct watering right through to the root mass (light watering will only hydrate the fronds and turn them green giving the illusion that the job is done). However, the heat lamps soon dry this water off, leaving the plant still starved of deep hydration (this is the biggest killer of live moss in the heated terrarium). Rain and mist systems can be a real asset and can help to save the keeper hours of maintenance. In some of my own Dendrobates enclosures, the moss has grown well along the floor, reaching into the flowing water reserve. I have noticed that, in the systems where it has been allowed to 'dip into the water,' these mosses display the highest levels of green and seem strongest or most robust in terms of transplanting. This action does, however, use more of the water in the reservoir, meaning this requires almost daily topping up.

'Not all moss is the same...' Do not fall into the trap of thinking that the branded dried or even bag of wet moss from the local pet shop will magically spring back to life and grow like a weed. In many

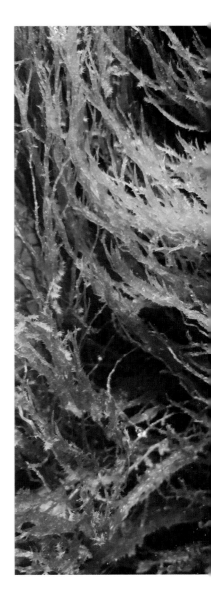

cases, this just does not happen. My experience with so-called 'live' sphagnum moss is just like this. It may be 'live' on paper but it does not seem to stay as such for long, nor have I ever been able to get it to proliferate as a sole source of moss. It does, however, have a use if a sustainable source can be found and that use is within humid hides, laying containers, and when used as packing for animals in transport. It will not, however, grow and stay a nice green colour like *Dicranum sp* or *Vesicularia dubyana*. You also will see in garden centres and other plant sellers a rather attractive and very brightly coloured large variety called 'reindeer moss'. This is usually a dried and dead moss that may have been died or painted bright green or red. As such, it will not grow and can play no real active role inside of the system of Wild Re-Creation™. I have seen plenty of keepers use it, but I must say that I worry about the chemical content of the colours used.

Cushion or pillow moss of the *Dicranum* family seems to do very well, as will live rolls of Carpet moss. You could use *Mnium hornum* (Carpet moss) and *Rhtidiadelphus triquetrus* (Electrified cats tail moss) or whatever is similarly available in-store inside of your own county. I buy my supplies on harvested rolls that are very similar to 'grass turf rolls' from the reptile industry here in the UK, and I know that a similar facility is offered around the rest of the EU and USA. You will, however, find that these rolls

Ants can be a particular problem I find in terms of not being actively predated upon by every species and then going on to damage plants."

of harvested moss contain a plethora of live invertebrates and eggs. I have found ants, springtails and woodlice, and all sorts of interesting things, within the rolls. There is, of course, a risk of snail and slug eggs, and I have lost a few plants as had to remove the odd offending slug from the vivarium when spotted. Again, the eagle eyes of the keeper are very much required to ensure a level of balance and ecological harmony inside of the system. Ants can be a particular problem I find in terms of not being actively predated upon by every species and then going on to damage plants. (This is in stark contradiction to springtails of which I have seen numerous species of reptile and amphibian both great and small actively and regularly consume.) The inclusion of live moss therefore is considered essential but requires some thought. There is very little soil to remove and, due to its fibrous nature, soaking alone does not remove all predators; however, it should have any loose earth shaken free and be immersed in tepid water for around five minutes before being planted. This will reduce the risk of harmful pest propagation. It is then up to the keeper to intervene and remove pests quickly until stable.

Vesicullaria dubyana or Java moss also is a good choice for forest systems with flowing water or pools. This species has been almost farmed for decades for the aquatics trade as it will even grow quite well under water. It also will grow terrestrially, but of course requires a very humid environment to do very well, I find. It does have a lush green colour and long tendrils. For many of us, it was with Java moss where the first frustrations started. Images of lush green enclosures, with thick carpets of moss, are very inspirational, attractive, and easy to find. Java moss also is very affordable and easy to obtain; however, due to its specific care and water requirements, it often disappoints, proving why the correct choice of moss species is indeed so vital.

Moss also needs trimming. I find that to encourage good growth, where giving the top few mms of carpet moss a trim down once or twice a year really seems to help. Of course, over-trimming can damage the moss, as can animals digging within its core, seeking to deposit eggs. These are all basic limitations that are easily overcome with a little bit of care and active maintenance. There are some fantastic print and online resources that deal with the subject of moss. I have found some particularly good information in books and on the 'terrarium' forums and groups. By terrarium, in this case, I refer to those with no live animals—the 'bottle garden' keepers.

Moss also can be used both to brighten up and to complete the aesthetic look of a modern enclosure. It also can have a very useful function. As such, we must keep an open mind and once again appreciate that everything we add into our systems must be safe and measurable and also must have a positive use and an interaction with the rest of the system. Decoration or 'landscape' should always have a function! Moss provides welcome cover, which is a core function in and of itself. It helps to maintain and to regulate levels of available humidity, and further provides soil nutrients as part of its own lifecycle.

Do not limit yourself and think that moss can only be grown in super wet or very humid systems; this simply isn't true. With a little bit of extra work and regular maintenance, there are mosses that can be grown in many species-specific enclosures. Okay, we may never find a species of bright green moss that can be grown in our super-hot desert terraria, but for those of us with forest- and jungle-dwelling species, its inclusion and growth can be easily facilitated and appreciated.

Planting Requirements and Suggestions for Easy-to-Grow Species

This book is not a directory for vivarium and terrarium plants; rather, it provides a starting point from which forward-thinking keepers can begin their journey into Wild Re-Creation™ through Bio-Activity. The subject would take years to document and further would require hundreds of pages of text and thousands of images to do correctly.

My goal, in this regard, is to provide an overview of the theory and accordingly to stipulate the tools needed to start your journey towards Wild Re-Creation™ through Bio-Activity. There are, however, already plenty of fantastic print and online resources available that can help you to make the right choices of exactly which species of plant to include within your own system. There are some stunning Victorian and Edwardian botanical reference guides that can be used alongside more modern resources to make good informed choices. I have found many of the older titles for just a few pounds on internet auction sites. It is also helpful to read about the origins of a species of plant before too much selective breeding occurred so as to provide us with the plant that we see today.

I will do my best to lay out just a few of the more common species or groups of plant that are widely available to us as keepers in the present time. I also will provide some basic hints towards their effective care. I will suggest where they can be used, along with any negatives to their inclusion. Please do, however, along with your Bio-Active goods supplier, ask which species of plant are available at that time and then once again check the suitability of these plants for your species of animal and inside your system. Due to the risk of direct predation from our animals and the live-foods that are used—and, of course, in mind of the transfer of the gut from predator to prey—species with a known level of toxicity must be avoided at all costs.

Remember, planting, much like vivarium decoration, is a long and relatively complex process. For many of us, it is all part of the fun. It cannot be rushed into and corners cannot be cut. We, as keepers, need to choose live plants that will help us to cater to the wild needs of the species that we keep. We have to choose plants that not only carry out a functional job but that also will offer security and enrichment for these animals and will remain attractive for the keeper. We usually would need to pay attention to planting at every level of the enclosure from the substrate upwards into the canopy, and we will have to choose species of plant that will thrive in our own system rather than allowing them to wilt and die quickly due to poor choice. As such, you should not expect to re-create that stunning enclosure that you may have seen in-store, at the zoo, or online on day one. Many of these systems are many years old, have a bank of electronics catering to their every need, and have reached a level of maturity that cannot be simply copied. You should expect to have a feeling for the kind of design or style that you wish to achieve at the start, add the plants in on a slow and gradual basis, be prepared to wait for certain plants that you want to come into stock or even season, and then sit back and relax as it all grows in. Live planting is fluid, enjoyable, and can really help to 'scratch the itch' of the creative person.

Wise choices must always be made with any inherent limitations kept at the forefront of thinking. Grasses and aloe plants can be grown in arid systems, as can the attractive and mesmerising 'rose of Jericho' plant. Some species of tillandsia also can survive in the hotter and drier environments. Reversely planting these more arid species in a forest enclosure would result in the very quick water-logging of the plant—and almost certain death. As an example, the rose of Jericho plant (*Selaginella lepidophylla*) I find simply moulders and dies if hydrated for long periods. It seems to require a cycle of becoming almost desiccated and then hydrated in season to do really well.

Animals also will dig underneath and they will consume plants. My own eyed lizards have a complicated network of tunnels underneath the substrate in their enclosure and, as part of this tunnelling process, the live plants become dislodged. So, like every good keeper and with minimum fuss, I have to re-plant the plants and, if they have been eaten, replace them. This is all pro-active maintenance. Climbing species, such as Pothos and Wandering Jew, can be grown in almost every system and therefore can be used in systems where live plant growth historically has been a struggle. These plants tend to add a flash of green very quickly, and can be used as shade and as quite sturdy vines for species that require them. There really is a plant for everyone.

A note with regards to herbivores and tortoises: this is a group of animals that, by definition, will consume or try to consume any plant that we make available to them. Does this then mean that it is a waste of time seeking to provide live plants for them? In reality, every animal is different and, as such, good choices need to be made per keeper. I have met more than one adult male green iguana that will willingly destroy with both mouth and arms any live plant that they see. This can lead to huge expense over time and a level of frustration that can only be understood by iguana keepers. Having said that, I would still rather see a large vivarium planted with banana, sturdy tropical trees and hibiscus bushes used for the green iguana than no live plant being provided at all. Yes, the iguana would consume parts of the plant as it should do, and yes this would require extra work on behalf of the keeper—but *that* is animal-keeping, I am afraid. Another method that can be used for the more destructive examples is a hybrid of the theory; this would simply mean using dried natural logs and branches screwed to the walls to create climbing and basking areas. Live plants then are grown in between the frame or even under small sections of aviary mesh, which can offer a good level of protection for the plant. I remain convinced, however, that the well though-out provision of live plants for these species remains a great idea and will allow the animal to live in and benefit from the core theory of Wild Re-Creation™ through Bio-Activity.

Tortoises present a very different issue indeed. I have a real soft spot for our shelled friends, and am convinced that many of the historic health and metabolic issues have been caused by a lack of dietary variety and a lack of exposure to the sun to the wild or required index. We can, of course, easily cater for their exact solar requirements per species now with the advent of clever UVB projecting technology, but many are still missing out on core nutritional provision. I firmly believe that tortoises should be allowed to dig and burrow; they should be allowed and encouraged to tear whole plants up and consume them 'roots and all'. It is here, in the natural and wild-like consumption of the roots and stems, that I believe many of the earth minerals—and, indeed, B vitamins—are ingested. This, to me, is the provision of a core requirement to their evolution. It does mean that live-planting indoor enclosures for tortoises can be extremely frustrating. But there is an answer.

Firstly, there is no reason whatsoever as to why tortoises cannot be maintained indoors as Bio-Active. The care principles of the theory remain the same. We can use mineralised, organic substrates and we can maintain a variety of substrate positive custodians. We then can easily maintain thermal and photo-gradients to suit any species, and we can adjust and maintain the correct levels of humidity. Long-term live-planting, however, remains an issue that requires serious thought and a little bit of extra work. In truth, you will not be able to maintain a long-term, landscaped enclosure with perfect planting. Our shelled friends will soon, and with great glee, ruin your every effort and hours of hard work. We can, however, grow safe and robust grasses and safe-to-eat flowers and, of course, vegetable plants. Trays of seedlings can be grown on the windowsill or in the greenhouse and then can be transferred and planted inside of the enclosure. Yes, most will simply be eaten or trampled on, but those that are allowed by the animal to flourish should go on to do fairly well if the enclosure is large enough.

Some keepers even grow these flowers in wooden or rattan baskets, and seat these down when the flowers appear into a pre-dug hole in the substrate. Another method that also caters to core Bio-Activity through the circulation of nutrients in the soil is to grow safe to eat plants under a series of wire cages inside of the enclosure. The plants are protected from over-grazing and from being trampled upon. The plants are able to use the animal waste as food as per the theory and to turn that into growth. As the plants grow, they will start to spread out through the mesh of the framework cage and then can be grazed upon without permanent detriment to the mother plant. Care should be taken to select a safe mesh; zinc-covered mesh presents a health risk to all.

Yes, there is a level of compromise to be made here and yes there is an extra degree of work, but this will help you to provide for your target species going forward and it will be worth it.

Tools

E very gardener needs tools, and there is no exception in the art of maintaining Bio-Active, live-planted enclosures. We may not require access to power tools or the traditional powered garden devices, but there are a few items that now can be bought fairly easily that will help you to care for the plants that you wish to grow and in order to facilitate maintaining the eco-system you have designed.

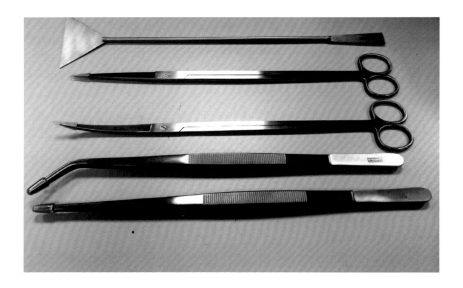

First off, you should obtain the very best quality pair of extra sharp scissors that you can find. Many plants will need cutting back, as in the case of Pothos, very frequently. Quality blades reduce the ripping and tearing of the plant fibres and allow you to carry out this maintenance with a lower level of risk to the plant. Bladed items should also be cleaned with a horticultural cleaner or heat sterilised, and sharpened between uses as required. If you decide to buy only one tool to help you, then please invest as much as possible in scissors. A good pair of pruning scissors really is a valuable investment that should last a lifetime.

Quality blades reduce the ripping and tearing of the plant fibres and allow you to carry out this maintenance with a lower level of risk to the plant. "

Tweezers: Tweezers will also be needed to help to move and manipulate plants and other decoration with minimum fuss. I find that the longer ones are easier to use. I always use stainless steel as the metal remains easy to clean and is a 'lifetime' product. Wooden or bamboo ones can be bought, but will need to be replaced regularly. I also use long tweezers with a silicone cover over the pincers. These are also useful with fragile things.

Dibber/spike: A good planting dibber or planting spike is a real asset. This basic tool will allow you to easily make good-sized depressions in the organic planting media in which new plants can be placed.

Mini rake: Again, a very useful tool for moving and straightening earth and digging in re-mineralising agents. They are also useful for removing debris and any excess faecal matter. Neat stainless steel ones can now be bought.

Small hand trowel: These can be found quite easily and also will allow you to both dig holes and grooves even in many confined spaces, but also will allow you to lift plants and, of course, take soil samples. Again, stainless steel is easy to keep clean.

Wire or string ties: These are a must for most of us. They can be used to train plants in the direction that you want them to grow and, of course, away from other plants. String can be good as it degrades over time.

Aquarium sealer: A good quality aquarium sealant is useful as this will allow you to affix air plants, Bromeliads and orchids onto another piece of suitable decoration. It also can be used to fix decoration in place (rocks and branches) and reduce the risk of harm due to accidental fall. The job of decoration-fixing should be done before the animals arrive or with the animals removed, and a good amount of time should be allowed for so as to ensure that any fumes have dissipated. Aquarium sealant is thought to be the safest option as it does not contain some of the added fungicides that are placed into household sealants.

Spray bottle: A good handheld spray bottle is essential for everyday watering and for increasing the humidity in the air. For large or multiple systems, a large 'back pack' version is also available.

Turkey baster: This common kitchen gadget will allow a keeper to withdraw any excess water from the drainage layer with minimal fuss. This reduces the risk of waterlogging and stagnation. This is an essential tool for those without a drainage tap.

Plant name tags: I will also include these here. Knowing the species of plant that you grow will help you to check species and the levels of growth, and of course emerging safety data on an ongoing basis.

Common Plants

I f you have ever tried to grow an orchid, tillandsia (air plant) or Bromeliad at home, you will have noticed that they tend not to do so well when planted in pots with the 'roots' covered in soil. This is because both groups are known to grow epiphytically; this means that they are commonly found above ground, fixed to other plants (trees) or rocks, with roots exposed. They are usually attached to this host plant/terrain but remain non-parasitical. They live upon/are anchored to this host, but do not take nutrients from them. Yes, they can sometimes be grown in soil—there is always an exception to the rule—but only really if the substrate particulate size is great enough to allow almost instant water drainage.

Bromeliads are best off removed from restrictive deep soil and then wired or stuck into the logs and branches. I find holes punched in cork tubes to be a very effective method for some species. I then place a thin layer of soil around the base of the plant and cover this lightly with carpet moss and bind with string or wire. This method I find provides short-term insulation and will increase the visual appeal of the plant fixing. The 'roots' on these

"Bromeliad wired onto bogwood"

plants are merely anchors and mist collectors; they need air and light to function correctly (depending on the species).

In terms of bromeliads, there are more than 2,700 species of 'Brom', with hundreds of these species readily available to us. They are found in almost every supermarket, high street and garden centre. They are available in all sizes, from very small to very large (*Guzmania sp*). They can be very colourful indeed, with blazing red and golden flowers. However, as above, they do not

"The same plant after 3 weeks strong lighting"

fare well in pots; they are also readily eaten by live-foods and they require high levels of light to truly thrive and to display the high levels of colouration seen instore for long periods of time. I have had the most positive experiences with the *Neoregelia* family. These smaller plants tend to blush deep red under good, high PAR full-spectrum lighting, grow and pup well. They also have a central pool of water that is used by many reptiles that choose to drink from them arboreally or are used as egg receptacles by many species of amphibian, including dart frogs.

(Do not forget that some amphibians seek out and deposit eggs and actively maintain young inside of these pools; they should not be allowed to run dry.) I also have had quite good success in very large tropical terraria with *Vriesea splendens*–a large, bold species with a flame-red, tall flower. One limitation I find with this group is ants. I have had more ants appear as if by magic with commercially bought broms than any other species of 'house plant'. Many of these plants are shipped over in large numbers direct from the South America; as such, I have never been able to correctly identify the species of ant or quantify any level of risk. As such, all potting media should be thrown away when new plants are bought and the plant carefully washed prior to being installed inside of the enclosure.

Tillandsia (larger air plants) usually are packed with no soil around them and, as such, can be easily wired onto branches and rocks. Those that are packed in a pot with soil should be researched to see if they do indeed require it or whether they should be un-potted and wired or stuck on once again. ,Again there are hundreds of species of this family available to us, and most of them are not only very safe but can be used in a multitude of systems. They will flower and provide good sustained colour. They are simple to care for and prefer to be misted rather than directly watered. In fact, the collection and study of this group can be just as all-encompassing as the collecting and study of the animals themselves! These plants need good air circulation and should never be allowed to become water-logged. They require dappled but strong levels of light, and can be fed with a suitable, organic mist fertiliser. Look for *Tilandsia fasciculate, Tilandsia bulbosa, Tilandsia bergeri* and, of course, the famous 'Spanish moss' *Tilandsia usneoides*, which can be used to drape over large pieces of wood and rock even in arid-type systems. As long as they are misted each day, they still tend to do well.

(Smaller) airplants, on the whole, are very easy to grow, of course, as they simply need a source of light and humidity. They can thrive in all kinds of system if you take time to choose the species that is correct for your needs. Once again, they are wired or stuck to branches and other decoration. They usually will arrive inside of a plastic bag and can be stored like this for many months. Many very good guides are available with regard to this intriguing group. They are very handy for providing delicate planting and colour towards the upper reaches of the system.

Orchids will also throw up thick roots above ground, and this is vitally important as they have to collect moisture through these thick and sometimes quite fluffy roots. These roots also need a source of light—again, another reason to never try to grow orchids inside of solid coloured pots. The most common species of orchid offered for sale is from the *Phalaenopsis* family. These are farmed in vast numbers. As such, I suggest that newly acquired plants are washed and placed in quarantine for a short period just to make sure that any chemical trace has been dealt with. Orchids can be included into most humid systems, to add into the system a splash of instant colour and a sense of the exotic. Some do fairly well and some will drop their flowers almost overnight when first bought. You then have a year of looking at a bare stem before more flowers may grow. Having said that, however, an established and strong orchid will readily flower, and this flowering season can last for two to three months at a time. They do need feeding through the provision of a propriety 'mist'. If you can find an organic variety, you will need to be sure that it is indeed reptile- and amphibian-safe. Please check with the brand before use. You also could look at the other members of the *Dendrobium* and *Bulbophyllum* families. The negatives are the plants' willingness to drop its flowers early in the first year. I find about 25-30% of the plants purchased end up expiring also, so work with the species until you find one that is both safe and robust enough to perform the job you have for it. There are indeed plenty of options. I do like the level of choice they offer. They can be planted high or low, and even moved around to suit until you are happy with the appearance

"A commercially grown Phalaenopsis orchid"

of your enclosure. When you are happy with its position, leave it well alone or it may not go onto flourish.

Cryptanthus rubens is one of the Earth Star family. These plants are related to .Bromeliads but can be wired onto decoration or planted directly into well-drained soil. Personally, I find that they fare much better and will turn a wonderful shade of deep blush red when wired onto branches with the roots covered in soil and then wrapped in live tropical moss and placed directly under a

"A good example of a blushing Earth Star"

very potent source of light. They can flower but rarely; they will when settled, however, 'pup'. To pup is the expression used to describe plants that almost seem to be able to clone themselves by growing a separate and transferable plant from within themselves. Bromeliads, tillandsia, orchids and *Cryptanthus* species all have this ability. The *Cryptanthus* family really are a delight to grow and to view. Watch out for over-watering and livefood predation. These plants will start to brown from the edges of the leaves, and this will spread throughout the leaf when over-watered or burnt by strong ultraviolet. The plants should be removed from the soil and allowed to dry for a short time as soon as possible or it will die. Quite a few specimens can be used even in fairly small enclosures to pick out the colours of the other plants and to increase the levels of colour themselves. A real must for the more established system.

Bird's nest fern, *Asplenium nidus*, and others in this family are also known as the bird's nest fern. These are robust ferns that can be grown in the substrate or in a similar fashion to the Earth Stars, but with more organic soil packed around the roots. They provide fantastic cover and will grow quickly and strongly. I find that using a mix of ferns like this one will also send roots deep into any water residing in the drainage layer, which is very quickly utilised. They remain thirsty and require high levels of full-spectrum, high PAR light. I also use *Adiantum*, *Athyrium* and *Davalia sp* to provide thick ground cover in most of our forest Bio-Active systems. Watch out for both extremes of water-logging and over-drying. Locusts seem to adore them, and so care needs to be taken. I also find that they fare far better when the old, dead fronds are removed. If the colours fade or the plant wilts for no apparent reason, it could be a sign of being underfed. Try a good organic worm manure-based fertiliser around the roots. There are very few negatives surrounding this fern.

Heart fern, *Hemionitis artolia*, is a species of plant I have only recently started to use. The plant has fairly broad, quite hairy, avocado green leaves in a definite 'heart' shape. They do not like to be over-watered, meaning a well-draining substrate is preferred. They can, however, I find, tolerate quite high levels of heat. This is a plant that grows quite well and will replicate itself almost constantly. The sturdy leaves reach forward on thin, hairy, long brown stems towards the light. They can be planted in the ground substrate or planted in soil inside of holes made in logs arboreally. The negatives are that they are not very sturdy at all. Imagine balancing a saucer on top of a pipe cleaner and you will get the kind of idea. Animals walking over or amongst them will simply cause the plant to lay flat. They do seem to recover within moments after the animal has left and the constant sending up of new stems in most cases compensates for any fatal breakages. This is a plant that is well worth trying in your system. The leaves tend to grow larger as the plant ages, and the stems will become longer in taller enclosures as they reach the light—a very nice if not quite strange-looking plant.

Pothos, *Pothos scindapus*, is an easy-to-find and very easy to grow plant. This is a plant that will trail like a vine or climb up towards the light with a vigour that is only matched in fiction. Every leaf can be cut at the stem and placed in a cup of water, whereupon

"Heart fern"

it will sprout roots and become its own clone within a day or two. This is one plant you cannot do without. They can support fairly heavy animals and are fantastic for the smaller chameleons to walk along. They can now be bought as being pre-trained up a mossed pole. This pole can be planted into your enclosure where the plant will spread outwards and upwards almost before your eyes. One thing is for sure: you will never be without some of it growing somewhere in the enclosure or around the house. There are very few negatives. The plant seems to thrive in all light

"Creeping Pothos"

levels and in all soil types; it will even, as stated, grow in a cup of tap water! One down side is that you will have to trim it out quite frequently or it will take over the entire enclosure and starve the other plants of light and nutrients! It also can be used by the species of leaf-folding frogs where they will place their eggs.

Wandering Jew, *Tradescantia sp*, in a similar way to Pothos, is a climber and a creeper, but has many more leaves than Pothos. Different species display different colours and leaf sizes. They can be grown in the substrate or in pots, and hung at the top of enclosure and allowed to grow downwards as a wandering cascade. They seem to grow well in almost any system and will spread very quickly indeed. As such, regular cuttings can and should be taken. Push these cuttings back into the soil and watch them take off once again. Live-food will seek them out but they grow so quickly that this should not be a long-term problem. This species also can be grown from water pools and, as such, will help to keep standing water fresher for longer, even if a filter is being used (which it always should be, ideally with a suitable UVC steriliser).

Snakeskin plants provide splashes of colour at the ground level with the inclusion of the *fittonias*. These very attractive little plants are often available as small seedlings that will need a period of growing on. I find them quite fragile, and they do appreciate a lower level of light and very good drainage. In fact, excess water will cause these plants to wilt and die almost before your eyes. They are also very prone to predation from live-foods and the odd stray slug—one of those plants that you have to have in the system and always look stunning at first; a real boon when settled but hard to get going, I find. The negatives include its intolerance to excess water, fragility of stems and its tendency to be eaten. Cut away leaves when they have started to turn brown and reduce the drainage layer water level if they start to

"Just hatched a baby Pygmy chameleon climbs up into the world"

wilt. They also tend to bruise and break when heavy animals walk over them, and so they are best used for frogs, small chameleons, arboreal snakes and small arboreal geckos. A good organic, worm manure and mineral-based plant food can be a life-saver with this rather fragile group.

Dragon Plants, *Dracaena sp*, is the houseplant that almost every household has. Usually green and yellow or green and red. They are slow-growing and fairly hardy. They prefer high humidity around the leaves, but should not be water-logged around the roots. They can be grown as 'plug-ins', meaning that the root ball and soil is plugged into a suitable hole in the decoration, which then acts like a pot arboreally. These plants can really add a 'spike' of colour into the system. They are well used in Dendrobates collections when small but equally larger examples can be found, which can be suited to the larger species of snake and lizard. I have not found any negatives with this species.

Spider plant, *Cholophytum comosum*, is another mass-farmed species that is available in all stores pretty much all year long due to the vigour in which it grows and its ability to reproduce. This is one of the most common 'class room' plants due to its ability to thrive in even the harshest surroundings and its ability to clean the air. It can be grown at the floor or in the canopy equally well. It will constantly grow new 'satellite' plants, which then can be removed when large enough and replanted at will. They can tolerate fairly high temperatures and can survive in the more arid systems. They should be misted down daily, with the base watered well once or twice a month. Organic feed can be used every other month if required. This species is non-toxic, with many tortoise-keepers allowing their animals to graze upon it at will. It grows quickly and deserves a place in most systems. Cut away any brown leaves quickly to encourage sustained growth. When grown arboreally, it will cascade downwards as a sea of green and cream leaves. It can make for a real centrepiece when large enough. This is a species that is very useful also for small frogs, such as the reed frogs, who will rest and call from within its fronds. The only negatives are that plant-eating species will actively graze upon it, and it also can form quite a large ball quite quickly.

Boston fern, *Nephrolepis sp*, are big, bold quite prehistoric-looking plants. Light green fibrous leaves make this a real centrepiece or a plant that can be used around taller flowering species to enhance the colour and draw the eye. They tend to spread outwards and become quite chunky, rather like a cabbage, rather than grow upwards. They are a real asset in jungle systems. Frogs, snakes and small lizards alike will find shelter within its fronds, and with a small pool of water at the centre, with its ability to hold water in its folds, this plant has a real use. Very large systems can have many of these plants grown to create a real sea of green with a very important level of enrichment and hydration provision. The negatives are that the plant is actively grazed upon by live-foods, and it may need

"Fern"

moving around the enclosure to find the level of light it requires. Under-illuminated plants tend to be very dull and will wilt.

Ficus sp is available in every good store in many different shapes and sizes. It has been sold as a house plant for centuries—and for good reason. It grows, and even when mistreated it continues to grow! This is a plant can bought in a multitude of sizes, from a tiny plug right the way up to an architecturally designed small tree, reaching over 8' tall. As such, regular pruning and training may be required.

"Ficus"

I find that the plant prefers a 'little and often approach' to watering rather than flooding or being kept constantly wet. It can be fed by misting the leaves themselves and via the root ball, both with a reptile-safe organic fertiliser. This plant is especially good for large enclosures. It will grow and spread fairly quickly, and also provides very good leaf-scatter patterns of light. It has quite sturdy branches and will support animals up to the size of the adult mountain horned dragon, juv water dragons or small tree monitors. It is especially good for arboreal snakes that will wind around the many twists and turns to find a safe anchor point. This is a fantastic plant with many uses for the modern herpetologist. I also include the very sturdy and sometimes quite large *Ficus elastic* or 'rubber plant' in this section–probably the most famous general house plant in the world. It is big and bold and attractive, and can sustain the weight of quite large animals when grown. Large enclosures can be planted with a mix of Ficus and, of course, the cheese plant *Monstera deliciosa*. (The creeping figs or *Ficus pumila* are also a great asset. They can be grown along the ground or like spider plants, planted in the canopy and allowed to trail as a vine.) The only negatives are the sizes to which these plants can grow and the tendency for Ficus to drop a good deal of its leaves quite suddenly when it is not happy. If you start to see excess leaf fall, you will need to look again at its light provision, feeding and root hydration. New leaves should always be visible as a thin emerging bud close to where the old leaves fall. If these buds are not present, it may be a sign that the plant is not happy.

Hibiscus, *Hibiscus rosa sinensis*, can be thought of as one of life's superfoods in its own right. Hibiscus is largely suitable for human and animal consumption, and has been used for thousands of years due to its many reported medicinal and recuperative properties. Every part of the plant is edible and holds positive and high levels of nutrition for humans and other animals. It is a ready

"A small Mountain Horned Dragon resting in a small rubber plant"

source of Carotenoids and Vitamin C, which is helpful to reptiles during times of stress. It also offers a helpful level of Iron which, I feel, is somewhat lacking in propitiatory reptilian diets. It is high in Thiamin and contains good levels of broad spectrum earth minerals. The flowers and leaves also are water-rich, helping with continued hydration. The plant is a typical bush but can grow to around 6' in height if allowed to do so. This is a stunning plant that grows an abundance of large, brash and showy pollen rich flowers. The flowers are eagerly sought out by many species of reptile, including the green iguana and tortoises. (I would like to see what the Madagascan collard lizard and Madagascan iguana thought of them.) The flowering period is very long indeed outside even Western Europe, where 4–6 months of flowers is not uncommon and may even be elongated further still in a stable, heated and light-rich vivarium. They require good drainage and regular watering, as well as accurate mineral-rich feeding. They can be trained and pruned to suit the needs of your enclosure. Be prepared for your iguana to go mad when the flowers appear; they will be eagerly consumed and will do the animal the power of good as part of a full and varied diet. The flowers and leaves also can be harvested and fed as fresh or as dried to any and all herbivorous or omnivorous species. As examples, the bearded dragon will readily consume them, as will most tortoises. This plant is an essential inclusion into the larger Bio-Active system, and will live a long and fruitful life if the care is right. A removable protective cage also can be used over the plant to protect the leaves and flowers and also to prevent over-grazing during the year. Be watchful for invading insects and cut away the previous year's wood so as to ensure a blaze of nutrient-rich flowers the next. Yes, this is a big one, but is it worth the extra little bit of work in terms of appearance, enrichment and nutrition.

Prayer plant, *Maranta leuconeura*, is another broad leaf houseplant that is safe to use and remains attractive throughout its long life. The leaves fold up at night, hence the name. It is quite fragile in nature and will not sustain a heavy animal trampling all over it. They are beautifully marked and well worth the effort. These plants are available in a stunning range of colour variants from green and yellow to green and red. Choose healthy, strong plants with signs of new leaves developing, and one with a thick centre should be chosen. If the care is right, these plants will live for decades. We had one such plant in our family that lived for well over 30 years and was itself a cutting from a plant obtained soon after WW2. The negatives are that it requires careful attention when new and that it remains physically quite fragile throughout its life. Cuttings can be taken and generally do very well. As such, you can ensure that you always have a replacement or two should it suffer animal damage.

Elephants ear plant, *Alocasia polly*, is a species that I have only recently started to grow. It has thick, rubbery/waxy bicolour, heart-shaped leaves that taper off into a point at the end. They are fantastic as natural, live waterfalls, and seem to grow well in live terrariums. This species does not like big rises and falls in temperature, and should be placed slightly away from high levels of direct light. They need to be kept humid and should be well-watered. This species does flower rarely and will die off every year and return the next. It is well worth the wait! The negatives are that they seem to suffer with being under-watered or over-watered in the wrong way. The leaves turn brown from the tip upwards and decay quickly when old and should be quickly cut away. Having said that, however, they are always thirsty, especially when growing: I have one such plant that will visibly drain a pool of water over a 24-hour period. They do not like to be immersed in water as in with very wet soil but they do seem to appreciate having their roots in the pool.

Peperomia, *Peperomia verschaffeltii*, is a species that is widely available and always looks fresh at first. They provide good ground cover and require fantastic drainage and dappled light. A nice plant that does quite well when settled. Live foods tend to destroy them, and I find that any stray slugs may make a beeline for them. Good care and a watchful eye are required at all times.

Banana, *Musa balbisiana, Mornata*, is the Banana plant, which is a very big sturdy plant/tree that can be maintained in the larger tropical enclosure and will produce large, deep green leaves and stunning flowers in season. These plants have become fairly commonly available in plant centres and supermarkets alike, and therefore should not be difficult to obtain. This is not a species of plant that can be grown in small enclosures; some dwarf varieties can be found. They require a stable level of heat and good full-spectrum lighting of a high PAR for long periods. They remain thirsty due to the size of the leaves, and they respirate well. As such, they require both frequent watering and foliar misting. They also will strip out the substrate nutrients very quickly indeed. Targeted drip-feeding around the plant base maybe required. They can be very useful for animals to find refuge inside of and they make for a real hotspot of colour. Leaf-folding frogs and flying geckos, as an example, may find them especially useful for egg-laying. Old leaves should be pruned away at the base of the leaf to maintain continued good growth. The negatives are the potential sheer size: full-sized banana plants can grow to over 12′ high. Thoughtful pruning and species-selection is always required for this stunning and typical tropical-looking plant.

Parlour palm, *Chamaedorea elegans*, is another species that is very easy to find in a variety of sizes to suit vivaria of 18′ high and upwards. It can be found potted as a baby 'plug', as well as in giant pots around 4–5′ high. This is a species that can provide fantastic resting and basking places for reptiles and amphibians; indeed, even smaller arboreal snakes can make use of them. It is a safe and very easy-to-grow species that requires good full-spectrum lighting and well-drained soil. They do not like excesses of heat or draught, and so placing away from heat sources is advised. I grow mine under a full-spectrum plant-growth lamp but away from the heat source. They require both root-watering and a regular spray down of the foliage. They benefit from organic and fairly regular feeding. The modern Bio-Active system is ideally suited to providing for their long-terms needs. The negatives are that they grow quite tall and insects will destroy them if allowed to do so. New leaves, however, grow fairly quickly.

Baby tears or 'mind your own business' plant, *Soleirolia soleirolii,* is a fast-growing mat-like plant that will grow and grow. It provides very good coverage for ground-dwelling young reptiles and amphibians alike. It really does inject a splash of lime-coloured high greens into the system and requires very little special care. Plant the smaller, new plants away from sources of direct light and do not allow to become waterlogged. Some variation of colour can be expected. This species can be grown in most systems from the tropical to the humid savannah. This plant is a real asset for the Bio-Active keepers, and has very few negatives. In one of our own systems, we use this plant as a mat of low level coverage for hatchling pygmy chameleons. The babies tend to stay within its protective layer for the first few weeks of life. Another observation is that the springtails seem to congregate around the soil under the leaves of this plant, allowing young lizards to feed almost constantly. If you wish to have a vibrant green matting inside of your enclosure and are finding live moss a real challenge, then baby tears may be the plant for you. It is certainly much easier to maintain long-term.

Juvenile Golden Mantella in 'Baby Tears'

Peace lily, *Spathiphyllum wallisii*, is the typical peace lily. Keep away from high heat or cold zones. Do not over-water and plant in a well-draining mineral rich substrate. These plants are easy to find in-store and flower almost all year long. Some confusion exists as to its toxicity, however; as such, it should not be used with species that actively consume plant matter. Live food also should be discouraged from eating it. Nonetheless, many thousands of keepers use this plant to inject colour and maintain a long season of flowering, and have done so for years with no adverse results. I myself advise caution.

> Although insectivorous plants can look very nice and add in extra colour into the upper reaches of the system, they do pose a risk to smaller animals."

Insectivorous plants—plants such as the pitcher plants and venus flytraps—*dionaea muscipula*, can be a real asset for jungle-system keepers. They can help to mop-up any access of nuisance fungus gnats or functioning fruit flies and, when properly placed, can really install a visual sense of the deep jungle. The species belonging to the *Sarracenia* family seem best placed for our use. Be careful with very small animals, however: it is quite well-documented that a large specimen could entrap and consume small reptiles and amphibians. You also may need to target-feed the plant with feeder insects; this is fairly easy with long tweezers and the odd cricket. They require dappled light and benefit from a constant level of humidity to be able to make and maintain new pitchers. The pitchers can be helped out after traveling or after being knocked by animals by having the tube a quarter refilled with clean, room temperature water. Before so doing, however, seek professional advice if incorporating these into your systems as, although these plants can look very nice and add in extra colour into the upper reaches of the system, they do pose a risk to smaller animals. Great care should be taken.

Mother-in-law's tongue, *Sansevieria sp*, is another large group of plants that are particularly suited to the more arid and rugged terrain. They thrive on periods of low humidity and high light levels. They are available from very small 'plugs' right up to some species of this plant being over 5' tall. *Sansevieria trifasciata* is the most commonly available, but I also like the tall, rounded fronds of the *Sansevieria bacularis Mikado*. These plants can be grown with good spacing, and the species mixed in the correct height arid enclosures. They make for a nice blaze of high green when grown alongside the *Aloe*, *Harworthia* and *Echeveria* families. These plants are large and bold and razor-sharp. Care must be taken. In truth, our animals seem to be fine around them: it is the keepers that tend to suffer. Do not underestimate this plant: *S trifasciata* can replicate itself via standard creeping rhizomes. It has a stunning flower, and has been noted as extremely effective at improving air quality. They can tolerate periods of little or no water and high temperatures, and may even benefit from doing so.

The Succulents is a huge group of plants that survive in more arid systems. They are found growing in many 'rock gardens' and bottle gardens. They stay fairly small and grow very slowly. They fare quite well with simple substrate moisture and infrequent watering, and are ideally suited to use with the leopard gecko and any species from a similar climate. The *Aloe*, *Echeveria* and *Harworthia* plants I also include in this group. I have attempted to grow them all in well-draining soils with quite mixed results. My own eyed lizard enclosure has a very deep substrate and is very hot, bright and UV-rich, with an index of 1.5–2.00 at the floor, raising to 7–8 under basking. Even for these highly adapted plants, this is a harsh life. Planting away from direct heat and away from the constant digging of the females is required. Try the following: *Aloe aristata, Aloe mitriformis, Aloe squarrosa, Harworthia margaritfera* and the many *Echeveria sp* that are available. Wet roots or pooled water in plant centres will kill these plants off almost over a weekend. Many shops also sell *Sedum burrito* as part of arid system sets. I find that this species fares much better in more humid, woodland-type systems, but seems very attractive to live-foods.

"Planting for an arid system may not be as hard as once thought"

Living stones, *Lithops sp*, are a hardy and enthralling species of succulent plant. They have solid, fused leaves that resemble pebbles. They are found in dry, pebbled areas, where they blend in perfectly. They originate from Africa and, as such, prefer to have a very strong, PAR-rich source of light. They will tolerate very high heat gradients and require very infrequent watering. They can flower if the care is right, with the flowers very attractive and almost daisy-like. Over-watering is fatal for these plants: they, like many true arid species, collect water as moisture from early morning and evening mists; care needs to be taken. They can be grown alongside *Harworthia* and such like species. Being so readily available and generally affordable, the living stone is the perfect choice for the more arid species. Larger lizards may trample over them, as can heavy snakes; however, they are fairly resilient, and it is not often that fatal damage occurs. Nonetheless, there is the need to be thoughtful when planting, positioning them away from the usual 'tracks' of the animals.

Aloe vera, *Aloe barbadensis*, has risen to an elevated level of fame in recent years due to its long list of reported medicinal properties. Quite honestly, not many other items are quite as valuable for treating cuts and burns in humans and animals alike. This is a plant that is simple to grow and will thrive in high-light level arid systems. They need infrequent watering, and the soil should be allowed to dry around the base of the plant prior to watering again. The leaves should grow directly upwards and feel very ridged to the touch. If the leaves are curled or spongy, the plant is under-hydrated: if the leaves grow horizontally or at an angle, it is probably reaching for more light. Small pups should be removed and re-planted when large enough or otherwise they will steal nutrients from the parent plant. I find that escapee Morio worms gravitate to the plants and eat it from the base upwards. Healthy plants should grow well and produce young plants that can be placed all around the enclosure. This species is especially good for arid species such as the bearded dragon, and is more than safe for the animal to consume.

Grasses, many of the ornamental Mediterranean grasses, will grow well even in arid systems. They can be trimmed down and require very little water. Many species in the group can be thought of as a safe source of food for reptiles also. They are also quite helpful, I find, but only 'IF' the drainage provision is good enough for use with the African reed frogs that will then sit and call in between the long stems. As with all ornamental grasses, you must treat them quite poorly for them to truly thrive. Cut the tops down for extra growth and feed infrequently. There are not many species available currently in the reptile industry, but I am assured that this will change. *Festuuca elegans* is a great place to start your

 Many of the ornamental Mediterranean grasses, will grow well even in arid systems. Many species in the group can be thought of as a safe source of food for reptiles also."

research—if a clean, unchemically treated source can be found. It may be easier currently to obtain seed from ornamental grass dealers. These then can be grown at will to suit the needs of your systems.

What is Soil?

The answer to this question is not as simple as one might expect. We cannot simply refer to it as 'mud' or 'dirt'. No, the 'soil' that covers our earth is a living, breathing entity all of its own. Soil is, in a very real sense, the 'skin' of the earth—a fully functioning organ, or it should be. This is why keepers that may have used a single ingredient substrate that has not been made from the natural soil building process will always struggle to maintain a truly Bio-Active system for any long period of time inside of a vivarium or terrarium.

Many of these off-the-shelf horticultural substrates have been designed for use in hydroponic systems for relatively short periods, where essential nutrients are literally and constantly directly pumped into the media through treated flowing water. This means that the media is simply there to provide a base in which roots can be housed or secured rather than ensuring that all of the essential nutrients are available through the soil itself at all times. If your media is made from coco fibre alone, for example, then you are missing 2rds of the component parts of wild soil; in other words, you are providing only one organic source and not mineral or any of the other multitude of organics. In this case, there always will be a limitation to growth and maintenance. Such a misunderstanding of a product use poses a potential serious imbalance, leading to poor growth and long-term nutrient-poor plants.

Soil is classed as having three main component types or groups; each and every element of the soil is vital, and without each one provided for in-balance, we have an imbalance and a potential long-term reason for decay. We also must realise that the soils that occur around the world are greatly different in their make-up, PH and density; each slightly different in each and every locality. The mineral content of the rocks around the area will greatly influence not only the PH of the soil but also its consistency (drainage), colour and nutritional potency. Soil, in and of itself, is complex and variable, and ever-building, -growing and -moving. Its component parts are truly influenced by the local area over vast periods of time, and also by the animals and plants that live, grow and eventually die there.

Soil is made up from the finely weathered (broken down) particles of the locality, and also washed-over stones and rocks (flood and river transit). We call this rock the 'parent' material. It is these rocks and their own mineral content that not only make up a portion of the soil, but also provide us with an insight into the

"EarthPro-EarthMix, Organic substrate"

minerals that can be obtained through the feeding and hunting process, per locality, per species.

Soil also contains a wealth of different sources of organic matter. This, of course, is made up from plant debris, decaying animals and faecal matter, amongst other local, wind-blown and flood-born organics. Again, the local species of plant and animal will have a marked effect upon the 'nutritional' quality of the local soil especially in the upper layers. We see that those areas of the world that have volcanic rock wash down or are on the site of historical eruption sites are noted as being some of the most fertile places on earth. The clue here is in the ready and bio-available mineral content of the parent rock.

It is incredible to think, when holding a handful of soil, that these solids, whether they be mineral or organic matter, only make up around half of its total mass. The remaining 50% is made up from water and air. Again, look to the mineral content of the local water systems. Air and organic decomposition gases also are a vastly important part of soil composition. This 'air' creates pore space between the particulates and is a vital component part of soil as a whole. Too much space between the particles and water will flow away too quickly, and the soil becomes useless, with too little space, and the soil and root systems cannot breathe and can become waterlogged and starved of oxygen. Having the correct pore space is just as vital to soil health as any of the others of the component parts.

(In a very real sense, soil can impede plant growth! This is why the true hydroponic systems work so well. The process of growing a plant in nutrient-laden and flowing water allows a plant to feed and hydrate through the roots, take up dissolved oxygen, and grow very much larger, very much more quickly. This is perfect for farming and in systems where quick growth is needed. However, as Bio-Active keepers, we are reliant upon the whole natural processes of life and growth to work in symbiosis towards the common goal of effective and natural provision for our captive animals.)

We then have the billions of microbes and inverts consisting of literally thousands of species, all working hard to turn the soil over, breaking down the millions of tons of organics into nutrients, whilst ensuring that life goes on in balance and harmony. This is indeed a vast and complex symbiosis of life.

Plants and animals require nutrition! Nutrition is not only classed as being plant- or animal-based food sources: we also have to factor in minerals. If a contained system becomes depleted of these essential minerals—by that, I mean as a soil or 'skin', living and breathing in a confined space that is not open to the elements—then the system or 'skin' will, over time, fail and die. Plants and animals constantly strip nutrients away from the systems in which they live and, as there is no flood, wind or rock fall to replace them naturally, depletion then will occur with the passing of time. The soil needs to be as accurately and as thoughtfully fed as the animals themselves are. I will say it again here: if we can keep an ecosystem, a habitat that is fully functioning at all levels and that remains potent and healthy, then we can keep any pertinent species of exotic animal that is pertinent to the size and type of the enclosure.

You therefore should pay close attention to the soil or substrate type that you choose to use in your own system. Organic substrates now can be easily found in-store for both forest and arid conditions. Simply look for the organic label; you then will know that it is truly safe to use with any species. Read up more for yourself on soils and their own component parts and accordingly try to understand how the differing parts interact with the world around them.

"A word of caution: please do not take soil from your garden or local area. You cannot be sure in these modern times that it has not become contaminated with something nasty."

The soil or substrate is indeed alive, and its exact supply and use is vital to the long-term efficacy of each and every captive system. Do not settle for any old substrate: this is the layer of which we build the foundations of our ongoing care systems. Get it right and your job will become much easier; get the choice wrong, however, and you will not only have a potential nutritional shortfall but you will create avoidable work for yourself in the long or even short term.

A word of caution: please do not take soil from your garden or local area. You cannot be sure in these modern times that it has not become contaminated with something nasty. Aviation fumes or poisons, pests, toxic plants, bacterial, fungal or viral infection that can effect both plant and animal are a very real risk. Some keepers state that they take soil from the wild and irradiate it in the microwave. Yes, that should sterilise the soil, but it will not remove many toxins. It will, however, kill off the essential microbial life.

How to Feed Plants alongside Animals

The move towards growing live plants inside of the majority of our enclosures is, as we know, both positive and beneficial, but we must never forget that a plant is itself a living, breathing entity all of its own. The plants that we use are not only meant to be decorative—that is, provide us, as the human keeper, with a slice of the wild and to act as a daily de-stressor—but to perform a vital and highly effective role in Bio-Activity and Bio-Availability. Plants, of course, have a defined set of biological needs and requirements and, of course, if these are not catered to thoughtfully, then the plant is likely to expire over time.

The good news is that a well-functioning Bio-Active system will help to provide for all the needs of the plants that we wish to grow. It is also true that live plants not only help to provide for our animals in terms of oxygen and water circulation—and, of course, food—but also that our animals can supply for our plants as part of an active and full circle of life. This is a close relationship that is easy to fall out of balance and is one that will need some human intervention within the enclosure.

Plants, as we all know, need access to water in the right way for its own species. It will need a source of earthbound nutrients or 'foods'. It will need, on the whole, good airflow to allow for effective respiration and also will need access to full-spectrum light in the right quantities. Again, we can our take tips from the recent advances in reptile science to see just how important light is for plants (see the chapter on PAR for more about the correct provision of energy from light for plants).

We then must seek to provide the best possible home for the plant. Some plants, like the bromeliads, of course, do not thrive if planted into soil but fare much better when wired onto branches to re-create how they would live in the wild. Others will need planting in the correct depth of organic substrate. Each plant should be able to access enough root space so that they are not all fighting one another for access to water and nutrients. It is better to space your plants well and then allow them to grow up than it is to overcrowd at the floor level. This then will allow the plants to settle into and to grow a good root network that will thrive for many years to come. One of the main causes of plant death is a restriction of root space and root dwelling predation and/or infection.

Plants need water, of course, and many benefit from a combination of root-up watering and regular leaf spray downs. The trick here, of course, is to monitor and balance our provision of water. If we have a system that does not allow water to be drained off naturally and our plants cannot utilise all of the water quickly enough, as we provide it, we then risk a pooling and eventual stagnation.

Stagnation often occurs in unmaintained and undrained pools, which allows potential harmful bacteria to proliferate in and around the water, leading to the soil becoming sodden. We then end up with a risk to both plant and animal alike. Built-in drainage taps are indeed a useful addition to live systems as they allow you to drain off excess water from an over-watered system, without having to break down the entire enclosure. Every system, however, also should have a drainage layer. This can be made up of pea gravel or commercial ceramic spheres. These allow you not only to see the level of spare water in your own system but also allows roots to have free access to the small amount of water available. As per the pathway of water, many of the soil nutrients also are washed into the drainage layer as water travels through the substrate. It is therefore important to strike a balance between adequate soil hydration and the needs of the plants. If the water is allowed to build-up quicker than the plants can use it, it then would have to be drained off along with the washed through nutrients. This could very quickly work to reduce any available minerals and other nutrients, and eventually leave your system quite depleted. In reality, the system would have to be well fed again or even restarted.

It is with nutrients that we must now concentrate. Soil nutrients are vital. They are vital to the health and wellbeing of plants and the animals that feed on the plants. They are vital to the direct mineralisation of animals. What do I mean by this?

Well, plants need food as well as water. In agriculture and home gardening, we use manufactured nitrogen and phosphorus-based sprays and pellets to try and put nutrients or 'food' back into the depleted soil so as to allow the plants to grow and flourish. As we all know, this happens even on land that has been over-used for long periods. In the wild, of course, these nutrients are provided for in an array of amazing and natural ways. Firstly, water washes minerals and organics down from the higher ground and onto the low grounds. These then collect in the ground itself as soils build up in mass over time and then become available for the plants and animals to utilise. Nutrients also are washed onto the land via floods and, to a certain degree, are found in rain. Nutrients also are made available to the eco-system via the organic breakdown of plant and animal matter, whether that be leaves or faeces, or otherwise through direct animal decomposition.

A whole army of micro fauna live and work all around us constantly. They are responsible for turning these organic compounds into a usable and ready source of food for the ecosystems in which they live. This is recycling at its very finest. I must now press a statement: when I refer to food, I do not refer to a sole source of food for plants. I believe that an ecosystem is a living and breathing entity, and that this entity caters to every biological function of every part of the system, from the massive to the microscopic. The process of a reptile or amphibian obtaining core nutrition direct from the earth is just as important to the process of total provision as providing a well though-out and gut-loaded ethical main diet. We also must not forget that many earth minerals and compounds, including many the Vitamin B group, are found in the soil. As an animal grabs hold of a plant or catches a live prey item, they no doubt will be ingesting parts of the ecosystem in which they live. Issues with natural provision only become problematic when one or more of these processes are allowed to get out of balance.

Do tortoises, for example, graze on ultra clean, mineral water washed spring salads in the wild or do they tear up whole plants and eat them soil-encrusted, roots and all? Do reticulated pythons find springs in the indo jungles and drink from them as a pure source or do they suck up water from any old puddle or watercourse they can find? Do amphibians seek out and live in mineral- and plant-free water or do they indeed fare well in an apparent soup of two parts hydrogen and one part oxygen, and what must be a million other naturel variants? This is not the first time I have explained the importance of the wild feeding process in this book, and it certainly will not be the last. It is entirely probable, as an example, that many of the Vitamin B deficiency problems we currently encounter, such as poor or partial shedding, is because we have not yet placed a high enough level of importance on the practise of obtaining nutrients from one's own environment.

With these statements, do I allude to what some may say is the controversial theory of self-supplementation in wild animals? Yes! And yes, I 100% believe that wild animals are not only able to but do sense a need for a mineral or minerals within their own bodies, and then go out of their way to obtain that item in the best, quickest way possible. Look at wild parrots and their need to ingest an amazingly rich source of minerals through the ingestion of clay. This is not purely a learned process to aid the pathway of digestion and toxin removal; they will be ingesting a rich helping of natural earth minerals and will be making use of those also. Look at some of the wall lizards as they lick salts from the walls they live around and then also look at some captive lizards as they ingest their substrates in a desperate effort to obtain Ca quickly in deficient systems. There is an action and an interaction for every biological and/or learned process.

We therefore can surmise that plants are as dependant on animals as animals are dependent on plants, even if we ignore the process of natural pollen transfer and fertilisation. It is in this process that we can help to cater to our plants as they live within our systems. As leaves fall and plants die, as animals pass their waste matter and roots around in the system, nutrients are built upon and made available. I am not for one second suggesting that the massive waste products of a large species should be left in a viv to stink and to fester, but if we have a full and active custodian base, a rich and deep substrate, and if we are on top of our maintenance, then the waste from most 'pet' species is not only more than assimilate-able into the system but will, in its own right, become part of the feeding process for the plants and, further on, animals.

In my own eyed lizard enclosure, waste is laid and becomes pretty much invisible within a day. This is an indicator that the system is working well and that disruptive human intervention at this time is not required. The springtails and other workers are doing their job, and the waste is then turned back into ground-bound nutrients for both plant and animal to reuse. The lizards are feeding the plants and the plants are feeding the lizards back. The substrate is fed and is active, and will contain a broad spectrum of vitamins and minerals just as it would in the wild. The custodians are plentiful and are, in and of themselves, a useful food source.

This process is very safe if we ensure we monitor the system at regular intervals. If the clean-up crew, for example, have died off or are not present in high enough numbers, the waste will not be dealt with properly or quickly enough and the system will fall out of balance. The presence of an unpleasant odour will be your sign that something is amiss and that you will need to step in and carry out thoughtful maintenance. More micro fauna will need to be added and waste cleaned manually until the right numbers have been allowed to build back up again.

Having said all of this, however, the soil is still likely to become depleted over time anyway. This is because there is not the full and normal process of natural erosion and exchange taking place. The risk is that the plants and animals take more from this finite source that they themselves can put back into it. In these times, the use of a natural and organic fertiliser or soil re-vitaliser can be used as directed. Organic mixes, based on organic volcanic matter, are particularly useful as they provide

"Volcanic rock dust"

broad spectrum minerals direct to the plants and animals and also help to further improve drainage.

The process of feeding plants is so closely linked to that of feeding animals that we should view them both with equal importance. If we can agree that the practise of keeping live plants—whatever pertinent species they may be is part of the forward-thinking reptile keeper's army of tools for ethical and effective husbandry—then we must also agree that the natural cycle of plant/animal

> A balance of the provision and management of these factors and a continued balance between the time spent on plants and animals that makes for a fault-free and effective system for the forward-thinking reptile keeper."

interaction is vital for each party. In truth, it is not the provision of an organic substrate that makes for a sustainable environment, nor is it the practise of leaving animal waste to be broken down by an effective clean-up crew, nor is it regular spraying nor the use of worm castings or volcanic matter that is the magic spell towards effective bioactivity. No, it is a balance of all of these factors: a balance of the provision and management of these factors and a continued balance between the time spent on plants and animals that makes for a fault-free and effective system for the forward-thinking reptile keeper.

Custodians

T he term 'custodian' is a rather simple blanket term used to describe all of the invertebrate (and also some vertebrate) species that can be used safely inside of an enclosure to maintain a healthy live and Bio-Active system. In reality, without the inclusion of custodians of some kind, you would not actually have a truly Bio-Active system at all; rather, the 'Bio' element would be missing. It truly is these important and sometimes quite microscopic animals that do much of the hard work for us. Another term that we could use to describe them is 'clean-up crew', although they conduct many more jobs than simply eating waste.

Yes, as we have seen, Wild Re-Creation™ through Bio-Activity is reliant upon the proper continuation of a whole series of natural, biological and, in some cases, symbiotic functions. We, as forward-thinking keepers, no longer simply rely upon the correct provision of heat, light and food to power our animals, but we place our trust upon a fully functioning and rather potent, all-encompassing micro ecosystem—a fully active and working slice of the wild. The idea, of course, is that every part of this system works together in relative peace and harmony to support the biological function of each and every other part so that the system, as a whole, becomes, in a sense, self-sufficient. (This is a driving force of nature—an equilibrium within the ecosystem. Of course confinement presents many limitations, including a lack of wind and food source movement. As such, a level of human interaction will always be required.) As an example, animal waste can be fed upon by micro fauna and turned into very bio-available nutrients for the plants and other custodians to feed upon. The micro fauna also feed upon and interact with the plants themselves: the apex predator may consume both plant and micro fauna, which then produces more waste for the micro fauna to consume and then go on to turn into more plant food. The wheel of life is ever-turning.

There are many species of custodian that can be safely kept together inside of a Bio-Active enclosure. Many of these inverts are now freely available instore at your local reptile shop and are also available by post online. Available species include springtails, tropical woodlice, white worms, earthworms, fruit beetles, small forest centipedes, and some of the smaller millipedes. Each species will conduct a different task and, as such, each species is equally as valid as the next. Some caution must be exercised, however, and a period of learning undertaken before any new species' inclusion. There have been reports of some species of woodlice literally infesting systems and eating the plants from the bottom up. We need to avoid frustrations like this, of course. I would suggest only investing in the now proven to be safe species from specialist Bio-Active system suppliers.

We can and should also open up this debate to a wider level. There are many other species that could possibly be thought of as 'custodians' in a very literal sense. In my mind, this 'term' simply denotes a species that works alone or with others to perform a useful task. In a very real sense, a small toad could also be described as a custodian as it would, no doubt, turn over the substrate and keep worm numbers in check—a very useful job indeed. In reality, however, using toads as custodians may be difficult to monitor and would be entirely unethical to use with any species that may predate upon the toad or the toad them, but it is my hope that you can see my point and why it is so important to open the debate as widely as possible so that we can make informed choices and go on to make positive changes as the hobby continues to evolve and to adapt.

I once saw a fully functioning Bio-Active system that had inhabitants placed at all levels of function. It was set up to mimic a working slice of Tanzania. The live substrate was made up of the usual springtails, tropical woodlice and worms as a useful and hardworking bio-culture, but also with the inclusion of a healthy breeding group of *Lygodactylus kimhowelii*, mixed species of reed frogs and Tanzanian millipedes. The system was heavily planted and large enough to afford every inhabitant its own territory. In a sense, every part of the system could be viewed as a 'custodian', as every part performed a useful function or had an interaction with the next. It may have been as simple as fruit fly or fungus gnat control or the way that the millipedes turned over the soils and allowed good aeration and consumed plant waste. It could have been the useful amount of faecal matter that the frogs produce or the upper level insect-clearing that the lizards performed. As you can see, this is, in all reality, an active and apparent homogeneity of nature but on a much reduced scale. (Human interaction, of course, is still required. In-viv parameters need constant maintenance, lamps changing, water levels and humidity adjusting, food adding, supplements administered and, of course, viv maintenance. In this case also, captive-bred young geckos had to be removed so as to not allow competition through overcrowding, predation of the young or potential inbreeding.)

Okay, so let's go back to basics and concentrate on only springtails for a short while. Firstly, what are they? Springtails are a well-known group of species of soil-dwelling invert. Interestingly, they no longer are referred to as 'insects' but rather as arthropods, with the subphylum of 'hexapoda'. They are found all over the world in and around leaf litter and are an ever-marching army of helpful workers. There are more than 6,000 differing species of springtail worldwide, with some species even crop- or 'plant'-specific. They also have a 'furcular' that is similar to a sprung-loaded arm, which locks into another 'limb' known as the 'tentaculum'. This is a typical spring and lock mechanism. The lock is released in times of danger and the animal 'springs' off to safety but without aerial control; hence, the common name of 'springtail'. They are wingless and, as such, cannot be found making a nuisance of themselves around the fruit bowl but rather can travel well themselves by walking and, of course, through the air after deploying the 'spring'. Most of the springtails available to keepers in the EU belong to the group of species 'collembola'. These really are the fuel to the 'machine' that is your Bio-Active system.

"Springtails feeding on EarthPro-CustodianFuel"

Springtails help to break down organic matter and then turn this into usable nutrients for both plants and animals to acquire. Springtails already will be included in the soils in which pot plants are grown and, of course, in and around wild collected branches. They are simply everywhere (they may not be available through irradiated or heat treated commercial soils but will soon colonise if introduced). We must however realise that starting a potent and functioning Bio-Active system will require many more inhabitants than will be available in the pots of our plants, and it will need them quickly. If using an organic substrate, springtails can be added in on the first day of set-up as there will be plenty of food available to allow them to reproduce quickly.

As we can see, it is necessary to invest in a few tubs of springtails to start off your system, but how many tubs will you need? Well, the truth is, nobody really knows for sure how many springtails there are even in a tub. From my own quite extensive testing, I have found the following system of inclusion to work very well indeed with organic substrates.

For a Bio-Active system of 45cm–60cm long and no more than 45cm deep, add in 3 large pots of springtails to your organic planting substrate on the first day, with only one pot of any other invert species that you decide to be pertinent to your system.

Mist the system down well but do not soak through. Leave for 24-48 hours and then add in the first of your plants, branches and rocks. Mist down well once more and then add in the leaf litter. Wait another few days so as to allow the system settle in and to watch for electrical problems before adding in any pre-quarantined livestock.

Then go on to add in one pot of springtails a week for just one month, then a further 1-2 pots a month after that as required. They will, of course, start to reproduce quickly, but remember also that they will die off naturally and be eaten themselves. The key to Bio-Active success is to have enough inverts available to break down plant and animal waste accurately and quickly. For vivs of 90cm or more long, simply add one more pot to the process above, i.e. four pots on the first day and then two a week for a month. If you decide against using a listed organic substrate, there may not be a ready source of food for the inverts, meaning you may need to feed the custodians with a good branded custodian food from day one.

Subsequently, you can quite safely sit back and watch the system settle down and continue to mature over time. When the ecosystem starts to maintain itself, you then can reduce the amount of extra inverts you buy and add in, but always according to the needs of your own system. Bear in mind that some reptiles and inverts will actively hunt springtails (pygmy chameleons will willingly hunt and consume vast numbers, as will most hatchling species) and larger species also will ingest large numbers as they grab hold of live, plant or defrosted foods.

Of course, this is an ongoing process, and more or even greater variety of this 'clean-up crew' will need to be added as and when the system requires. One test is to take a small handful of the viv soil and to spread it out in your hand. Can you see no or a few little white specs moving around or lots? If you cannot see them in numbers, you need to add more. As a rule of thumb, I try and count between 5 and 10 inverts per inch of soil when it has been spread out in my hand; any less and I add a single extra tub into the culture. Any more than 5-10 and I leave as is.

Coming back to my previous statement, we also must feed our custodians. Yes, plants require constant maintenance by the inverts and there should be plenty of animal waste around, but there will be times when this just isn't enough on its own to sustain and to allow your culture to reproduce in the vast numbers that are required. We have to feed our custodians just as we would feed our predators. There are now some very good custodian foods available in the shops that will not only help to feed the inverts but that also will make sure that they are actually nutritious in their own right. Another positive point to make here is that, even in relation to their diminutive size, springtails can transfer a useful quantity of calcium into the predator. As such, a food source that is rich in Ca will be required to ensure that they are nutritious as possible in their own right at all times.

A pelleted Custodian food, EarthPro-CustodianFuel

> " Many keepers also now add into their systems fruit beetles. These are highly colourful larger inverts and are a very good source of nutrition in their own right."

Whatever you decide in terms of custodian inclusion, you must know the processes inside out first. What species are safe to use and indeed mix with one another? What kind of 'look' are you after, and can that look or design be maintained well enough in the size and type of the system of your choice?

Many keepers also now add into their systems fruit beetles. These are highly colourful larger inverts and are a very good source of nutrition in their own right. They will reproduce well and need minimal extra care—just the addition of some fruit as a food source. The grubs will live and grow in the soil and play an active role in aeration via soil turnover and through the production of their own faecal matter. They then will metamorphose and crawl back up into the terrestrial world where they will either be eaten or be allowed to reproduce. The adults do not pose a risk to small reptiles and can make for a colourful and quite lively addition to the system. The grubs, however, do have quite powerful jaws, meaning caution should be exercised if used with ground-dwelling species. They can, like most beetles, fly, so bear that in mind before opening viv doors too widely.

Some keepers also add in certain species of cockroach. I am assured that they are safe and will live inside of the viv with no real maintenance concerns. My concern would be the risk of escape. We all know how good they are at that, and there is a world of difference between feeding a few grown on Dubias to a pet than allowing a species to reproduce in-situ at will. One can imagine the furore if individuals were found in the house outside of the enclosure. As with all livestock, care must be taken to provide for their needs in a safe and effective way. We must also ensure that we do not allow escapees of any species, be that pet or pet food.

Invert Control, Poisons and Culture Meltdown

P roblematic invert (pest/unwanted species) control and airborne toxins, both accidental and deliberate, all represent a level of risk to the continued overall health and functionality of a live and functioning system of Wild Re-Creation™ through Bio-Activity. Many of the off-the-shelf chemical- or even plant-based remedies for snake mite, for instance, will cause an almost instant meltdown with regards to custodian cultures, and also seem to pose a very real risk to both other 'pet' inverts and amphibians alike. One such spray I have seen working caused snake mites and their eggs to audibly crackle as the toxin quickly took effect. This is a very potent and easy-to-overuse treatment: being airborne via propellant gas particles, it can travel a far greater distance than many may realise.

There are many toxins that can and do poison our systems. These toxins or compounds may even affect our systems after even a brief period of treating a separate animal in the collection, even if it is placed in another room. There also is a very real risk from local airborne toxic compounds. Crop spraying in rural areas and even a build-up of traffic fumes in the cities all can have a potentially devastating effect, not only with regard to our live custodian cultures but also to our chosen animal species.

There really is no way to seal oneself away from the wider world and the many toxins that are constantly all around us, but nonetheless we can limit the level of negative exposure to our animals. As such, there are a few things that we, as keepers, can do to try and help protect our pets and the enclosures in which they live.

Fresh air is good—but not if it is laden with insecticides or herbicides. If you live close to farm land, you may wish to write to the local landowner and ask him or her to simply drop you a line if and when this type of product is going to be used. Most farmers are happy to help if you remain polite and courteous. You could then ensure that all of your windows are shut for that day and for a few days afterwards. This would act as a type of damage limitation. Surfaces can be wiped and curtains and clothes washed to further reduce any risk of contamination. There still will be a risk but you will have done all that you can to minimise that level of risk.

Some household sprays, cleaners and perfumes also have reported negative effects on both predator and prey. I advise great caution if using such automated room deodorisers, or hair and skin products in the same room as where your animals are kept. Anything that is propellant-based will allow particle-transfer in a very efficient manner. It is incredible just how far these projected particles can travel after being released under pressure, especially when household conditions are right. As a simple experiment, spray your usual body spray upstairs or in a different room for just 3 seconds. Then go back downstairs or into another room and see how long it is before you can start to detect the smell of that product. It will not take long, I can assure you. In this case, you are only really smelling the perfume that has been added to the product, and not the gases and deodorising chemicals that surround it. Can you see my point here?

Fumes from overheated non-stick pans are also well documented as having a negative effect upon avian respiratory systems and, as reptiles and birds are so similar, I once again advise great caution if using these products. Ceramic, copper or stainless steel maybe a better option going forward.

There also is a very real risk of total system failure from dog and cat flea and mite treatments. Many of these products are now so effective and, for such a long period of time, there is a risk from our household pets and their sometimes quite close contact to our exotics, especially soon after application. I am not for one moment suggesting that we should not actively protect our dogs from fleas and other parasites, but we must factor in a level of damage limitation for our exotic pets. Maybe treating the animal away from your collection and then maintaining an exclusion zone for a period of time afterwards would be effective.

There are many causes of systemic meltdown, each one as devastating and as frustrating as the next. In each case of system collapse, the system will need to be properly restarted as per the guidelines in the previous chapter. It would be best to have a thorough clean with an invert and reptile-safe product, such as F10, and to then buy a new substrate and then re-seed the system with fresh custodians. Wash all decoration if it is possible or, if not, buy new. It is with these more accidental meltdowns that the real frustrations lie. You did not action it nor ask for it, but it has affected your system and will take a large amount of effort and money to put things right.

Going forward, you should explain to your reptile-focused vet and reptile store specialist that you maintain a fully Bio-Active system before any treatments are given or used. Hopefully, this will allow them to recommend products and treatments that are safer to use inside and around your system. If all else fails and a 'toxic to invert' treatment simply has to be used for the long-term benefit of your animal, then treatment and recuperation should be undertaken at a separate location until such a time that it is safe to re-introduce. It may prove more effective and cheaper with regard to system re-start costs and, of course, the minimisation of risk to any other animals in the collection if the animal to be treated was admitted to the vet's hospital wing whilst the animal was being treated.

For some of us, the risk of toxic ingress is just too high to even consider keeping certain more fragile species. I have recently heard of a whole collection of tree frogs, for instance, being wiped out after the accidental exposure to a locally used wind-blown pesticide. In some cases, traffic or factory fumes could also have a similar, cataclysmic effect. This, of course, is difficult to quantify and, as such, each keeper should be happy with the species they choose to keep and be rest assured that the environment in which they aim to keep them will cause them no ongoing harm.

Humidity and Hydration

As previously pointed out, water is the glue that holds together all life. It is a potent and active force all of its own that not only sustains life through allowing good organ function, growth, digestion, assimilation and expulsion but of course every other biological process within a body. Without water, we simply have no 'life'.

In real terms, water, in some or another form, is found or can be measured pretty much everywhere. Even in the driest most inhospitable places, water is still available either in a sporadic oasis, a short way under the ground, or from cloud roll over in the morning and evening. We also find the most amazing adaptations to life in the most arid sectors of the world. Look at the Thorny Devil or Moloch of the deserts of Australia for a great example of localised evolution and adaption. This is a species that is perfectly adapted to make use of small quantities of standing water and mists through an amazing way of both obtaining water through capillary action and then storing it within its body for release as it has need over long periods. Other adapted species include the sandfish lizard and some of the desert geckos that have evolved in simply incredible ways of avoiding searing heat but also of finding water and using it to its full potential even in small quantities. Other examples would include the Chuckwalla and Uromastyx lizards, Desert Horned Lizard and of course Marine Iguana. Even some amphibians have developed highly adapted mechanisms for living under the sand in a kind of torpor or apparent suspended animation between times of rain in harsh desert or scrubland terrain. Difficult habitats and environments lead to a miraculous level of diversity in species adaptation.

"Once almost impossible to keep, the Horned 'toad' is now being bred in captivity"

We therefore must not only view water as a life-sustaining force but as a source of core nutrition. Wild water, whether that be from a standing source, spring or from rain, not only is mineral-laden but can be teaming with life of both flora and fauna. We cannot ignore how important macro algae can be with regards to providing useful nutrition. We also can see how water can help to maintain good levels of Ca in the diet through the mineral deposits washed from rocks and soils.

Water sources differ greatly around the world, of course, and we can see a direct link between gathered mineral content from spring and river sources and vastly increased land fertility. Of course, the soils around these flood plains and other super fertile areas also are available to reptiles who directly benefit from drinking the water and, consequently, through the additional nutrition provided by the local plants, insects and animals that feed off of these plants, and again through direct soil ingestion.

Humidity must be thought of as an important tool that can be used to ensure not only adequate but fantastic hydration. A system with a lack of humidity will not simply lead to poor shedding from dry air (this, in reality, I believe, is an outworking of an internal hydration, heat and vitamin imbalance problem) but can lead to poor vital organ function. We therefore must use the Bio-Active system theology as a tool to affect the correct level of hydration per species and at all times.

I pointed out in my previous book how some Agamids can rest within the burrows by day and, through this developed capillary action, 'drink' whilst resting or sleeping. What could be a better adaptation to life than being able to rest out of the way of direct danger from predators and away from dangerous levels of heat during the day whilst being able to nourish one's body while you do so? This may not be 'primary drinking', of course, but it does show just how important maintaining good hydration is at all times, or the animal would not have developed some of these awe-inspiring abilities.

Water aids digestion. Yes, we can correctly assume that, without the correct levels of hydration, the foods we feed to our animals cannot be made use of properly within the body unless the body is functioning at the highest level. We therefore should ensure that 'feeding' live-foods are not only accurately fed and heated before being fed onwards but that they are well hydrated also. Effective hydration allows digestion, assimilation and the complete use of nutrition. It also ensures that waste products are effectively and properly expelled from the body in a timely fashion. This, in and of itself, reduces the risk of harm and reduces the risk of impaction.

Water allows vitamin assimilation and use. Yes, it is essential that exact hydration is provided for to allow for the correct use and transit of the water-soluble vitamins, including the extremely important Vitamin B group. Being water-soluble, they are not stored in the body and remain free until used or expelled. To make full use of these important compounds we must ensure good hydration at all times in a way that is suitable for the species that is to be kept.

Water allows for an easy and full shed. Yes, there are many other parameters that need to be catered to, including the correct provision of heat and, of course, nutrition (B vitamins play an important role here) and it must be said the provision of good enough decoration to allow the animal to find sloughing places easily. Conditions like stuck eye caps could become a thing of the past, if we maintain the right level of humidity, hydration and nutritional supply.

Water also allows ease of reproduction. Yes a poorly hydrated female will still lay or give live birth but the whole process will be very much harder on her. This also means that the young may not have the very best start in life. We also have to look at the knock on effects of poor hydration through the reproductive cycles. Are the animals able to assimilate and store provided vitamins and minerals adequately, if not they cannot then pass these on properly to the young and will very quickly strip any reserves from their own bodies. Males that are seriously dehydrated are also effected with regard to the quality and quantity of sperm. Good hydration means fit parents and strong healthy young with the very best start in life.

Not all animals can drink easily from a bowl. I have covered this already, and it is a very important point indeed. A species such as the chameleon or many of the Asian Agamids are simply not set up to drink from standing water in bowls on the floor. They obtain water primarily from rain as it travels through the trees and bushes. As such, drippers and sprayers are essential items. Just because you provide a source of water does not mean that it will be properly used. Regular spray downs of the animal and its enclosure and the spraying of the substrate to increase long-term humidity will help greatly, as will adequately hydrated live-foods. I cannot stress strongly enough how important rain and mist systems are for arboreal animals. In reality, it is the difference between life and death in some animals. One example here would be the Draco or flying lizards. These highly adapted lizards have suffered historically in captivity; they seem to suffer terribly with stress but also from dehydration from a lack of rainfall and by not being fed the grub rich diet of which they prefer. Again, look to the wild habitat and habits, replicate this in a safe and measured way, and even these most delicate of species should become fairly easy to keep and to breed.

"Mountain Horned Dragon"

So how do we maintain effective hydration and humidity? Well, first we have to see both terms as one. Hydration is boosted by the provision of the correct levels of humidity. So, we provide water in as many ways as is pertinent for the species. Live-foods are fed and hydrated for at least 12 hours before being fed on. Salads and green foods are fed as un-dried. Water is placed in bowls for those species that will use them, and reptile-safe containers or even wide bromeliads are used for those that drink from water collected within the trees. Drippers, rain units and foggers/misters can be used, and hand spray guns utilised to provide rivulets within the plant work. We should carry this out pretty much each and every day. We then use a hydrometer to measure the levels of humidity within the substrate and accordingly adjust our provision of direct substrate watering until we reach the target level of humidity for the species in question. As such, humidity rises with the increased heat of the enclosure. The plants respire more water and the entire level of humidity rises inside of the enclosure.

We do have to be careful: a build-up of stale and stagnating water/humidity is not a positive force at all; in fact, it forms a direct and potential fatal bacterial build-up risk. Effective airflow and ventilation is the key here: we should not water more than the plants can utilise within a day or two and we must ensure that there is adequate gaseous exchange. Fans can be added to all systems and be programmed via timers to provide this service as part of a 'push/pull' system. These processes and actions are all part of effective Wild Re-Creation™. Each part of the technique replicates a wild action and interaction, and each part has uses and interactions within the system as a whole.

Water is vital—it is just as vital as the food and, of course, the supplements we use. As such, and as forward-thinking reptile-keepers, we really need to start to not only understand its importance but also how to ensure its correct provision at all times and per species.

New Viv Syndrome

I t seems rather crass and basic terminology, but there is such a thing as 'new viv syndrome'—well, in a sense. This term simply refers to the many wide and rather complex frustrations surrounding the set-up and maturation of a new system. It can affect us all and probably will to some degree.

As keepers, we tend to lump all of these apparent and sometimes quite angering problems together and pass them off as some kind of mythical attack against the system we are currently so desperately constructing. In a sense, sometimes it can feel like if it can go wrong it certainly will. In reality, there are a few similarities between some of the elements of this 'new viv syndrome' and the openly discussed 'new tank syndrome', which is very well-documented in print and online, and is largely due to a bacterial bloom in newly started aquaria.

There are many 'live' aspects surrounding the true Bio-Active system. Of course, it is not just the target animal we are trying to propagate alone: as Bio-Active keepers, we have to think of the entire system, right down to the macro level. We have to see the substrate as being 'live', which it truly is. It is with this microscopic world that many of the frustrations associated with 'new viv syndrome' occur. We must view this culture as being the life blood of the ecosystem, the engine that ticks away and ensures that everything is working as it should do but that this culture must be allowed to mature; it must be allowed to establish and to settle if we are to be sure of systemic balance. This will take time, and currently there is no overnight 'cure-all' solution. Again, this mimics a similarity to the initial start-up of an aquarium.

Keeping in mind that a Bio-Active enclosure is not simply a standard enclosure with potted live plants placed into it, nor is it one with a layer of coco fibre 'soil', it is important to recognise that it is a living breathing entity all of its own; accepting this will equip us with the correct level of expectation and allow us, as keepers, to work within the limitations of a system and the technology that supports it. Every live system has to go through a period of 'birth' and establishment. These systems are not perfectly in balance from day one, and we should never expect them to be. We can use the production of wine as an example. Crushing grapes and mixing the juice with water and sugar does not make wine; rather, it takes an interaction with yeast. Thus, over time, wine is produced. It is similar with Bio-Activity.

It is true, however, that, in a well though-out system that is well-fed with live cultures of custodians and with the foods they need to replicate quickly, that a live animal can be placed into the enclosure in a reasonable time after the system has been set up. We suggest that new systems are left for a minimum of one week to settle down and to start to establish before live exotics are added. In an ideal world, we would all be prepared to wait 2–3 months for the culture to mature, but not many of us have the patience for that realistically.

This quickened time frame will expose some frustrations that are above and beyond the usual set-up issues we have all experienced with the enclosure itself as well as with its electronic components. It is vital that a new acquired viv is set-up empty first and then the heating, control and lighting installed and run for a few days just to be sure that the viv itself is well-built and that every electrical aspect is working as it should. If not, it is then very easy to remove the frustrating defective or broken part and to seek advice or replacement. When you are happy that the basic system is working as it should, you then can start to add in the elements that will start the Bio-Active process. Of course, the waterproofing must be tested before the drainage layer and/or substrate is added.

The drainage layer goes in first, then the organic substrate, and then we suggest that the required number of springtails and other custodians are added and lightly fed. The viv then is decorated with natural stone and branches, and a number of plants and mosses are added. The whole system should then be watered in well and left to settle. It will be between Day 3 and Day 5 after you have lovingly designed the viv and planted it according to the needs of your target species that you will start to see any issues. Some plants may droop or appear to wilt (this may be due to over-watering, so check the water level in the drainage layer), and the decoration may need readjustment. This is all fairly easy design, building and maintenance. The most common cause of dismay for new keepers, however, is waking up one morning and finding a light dusting of white all over the substrate and over the decoration. Mould!

In a sense, this is a natural process. The organic substrate is live in and of itself. We then almost encapsulate it in glass or plastic or wood, and then hydrate it and often under ventilate it. We then add more micro fauna to the system, and organic consumption and gas production take place and water can start to pool. The net result of this live culture is, of course, 'life'. The substrate will bloom and this 'bloom' will spread and can look rather unsightly, but in a healthy system with responsible watering and good airflow this 'bloom' will disappear all of its own around 7–10 days later. In fact, it is a sign that the culture is indeed starting to mature and to become stable. It is a frustration but a frustration with which most of us have to persevere.

The 'bloom' should disappear without much in the way of intervention. If it does not resolve itself, it may be an indicator that you are either over-watering, have poor airflow or that the system is too rich for the plants you have introduced. More custodians can be added if this does not vanish all of its own. One thing is for sure: a well-set and functioning Bio-Active system should not have an unpleasant smell. If it does you have stagnation or some such unhelpful thing, you then should re-assess the system from the bottom upwards. A healthy system should have a slight smell of the forest about it.

The other main frustration surrounding a new Bio-Active system is condensation and water build-up. Again, with early vigilance in watering, this can be largely mitigated; however, it is quite normal for a new system to become very humid in the first few weeks. It will take a while for the plants to start to respirate properly and for the substrate and it inhabitants to absorb the water. As such, and especially with the heat associated with our hobby, the water vapour rises and collects all over the viv. In this case, it is important to use absorbent, disposable towelling to wipe off the excess water from the walls and glass on a daily basis. This will reduce the chance of unhelpful bacterial build-up and will allow the system to mature without having to fight further levels of stagnation. Increasing the level of airflow is extremely helpful: fans can be added or the doors left open if you have not yet introduced the animal and if it is safe to do so. Continue watering when required to maintain the soil humidity that is required, but continue to wipe away any excess from the walls and glass until the system has settled.

I cannot suggest strongly enough just how important it is to minimise the risk of stagnation. Stagnant water and cultures do not only smell bad but they pose a very real risk in terms of bacterial infection to our exotic animals. Respiratory tract infection, mouth and skin infection all can be linked to a stale and unstable system.

There does seem to be an almost magical day within the first two weeks after start-up when it all just seems to work. The 'bloom' disappears, the water magically stops running down the glass, and the plants perk up and start to colour up. It is at this point that the custodian quotas should be checked and the animal/s can be added in a safe and measured way. We must not, however,

"Just one of the Bio-Active enclosures at Arcadia Reptile HQ"

overload a new system. You may have a very big enclosure with space for multiple frogs, as an example, but putting in too many animals on the first day will simply risk placing a load on the bio-culture with which it cannot cope. In this case, the system crashes and you will need to start again. It is better to add in animals over a period of time and as the system matures.

As always, seek advice in plenty of time if things do not seem to go to plan. There is a vast number of very clever Bio-Active system-keepers out there now with dedicated social media groups and retail departments, catering for the ever-increasing demand of this sector of the hobby. Proactively seek advice and see your own system literally burst into life with the minimum level of stress.

B Vitamins

(Reviewed and updated from 'The Arcadia
Guide to Reptile and Amphibian Nutrition)

Vitamin B Group

The B group of vitamins all largely exist and work in unison with one another and with other core vitamins and minerals, working together for a common purpose; that is, to sustain life through vital organ and cellular function. They are one of those rare groups of compounds that can be thought of as both 'building blocks' and as the 'cement' of life. They are termed as being water soluble and, as such, are not stored within the animal's body for a long time at all, therefore meaning that they will need to be topped-up regularly through the diet, whether that be via the ingestion of food, water or, of course, via the environment itself.

Being water-soluble and removed from the body via egestion, we view the Vitamin B group as being 'non-toxic' (that is, the dose required to be thought of as toxic is so high that it is most impossible to provide for). They, as a group, are very important to the cycles of production and for the maintenance of red blood cells, bone and skin. They also have very profound positive effects on the brain and nervous systems, allowing good development and helping to build defences, thus staving off many of the now totally avoidable diseases that can befall the captive animal. We can see how potent members of this group can be in our own (human) healthcare, with large doses of Biotin being given to help promote the growth, health and strength of human hair, skin and nails.

As historical reptile-keepers, I believe that we have not at all placed a high enough importance on the group of compounds now known to us as being B vitamins. Historically, they have been chronically underprovided for in our care systems due to the move away from Wild Re-Creation™ and into more sterile, hyper clean, non-natural captive systems. Our animals also have been faced with an under-provision from the unnatural or limited diets we have offered them and a lack of potency within the broad spectrum vitamin inclusion into many of the proprietary supplement powders. B vitamins are vital to the long-term health and wellbeing of life. They are as important as Vitamin D3 or Vitamin A, or any of the other hundreds of natural vitamins and minerals that are ingested, assimilated and absorbed into the bodies of animals every day in the wild state.

B vitamins, in and of themselves, are not that 'magic bullet' or that 'cure-all', nor are they the answer to all of our concerns, but indeed they are a very valuable tool. They are active and potent, and remain vital to our broad spectrum approach to forward-thinking keeping. As we have already seen, modern reptile-keeping is based upon the provision of everything that a species needs to complete its own developed biological processes, thus ensuring the continuation of a genetic line without raising the risk of avoidable disease.

B vitamins are vital to skin, brain, blood, nerve and muscle health. Without adequate provision, we risk a far reaching and quickly manifesting descent into worrying levels of disease. Many of the diseases linked to a shortfall of B group vitamins also mimic the symptoms of other dietary shortfalls. As an example, a shortfall of Thiamine or Vitamin B1 can cause tremors and twitching, which of course is a sign of advancing Vitamin D3-related MBD. As you can see, it is vital that a vet's advice is quickly sought and bloods taken so that the right treatment can be given. If a keeper saw this twitching and shaking and increased dietary D3 and Ca, they would not cure the Thiamine reduction and, once again, would risk a chronic over-supply of D3, leading to potential toxicity. I have said it before and will continue to do so: we MUST always have a base point from which to work—an accurate starting point for medicine and its therapeutic action. If we know the cause of the issue, we can, with good advice, formulate a therapy that is not only effective but that is effective in the shortest possible period of time and in the most pertinent form for the species being kept whilst reducing the amount or severity of any side effects. We then maintain therapeutic efficacy without risking falling short of the maintenance dose and never escalating into the realms of toxicity.

This 'broad spectrum' of water-soluble vitamins are found in pretty much all the same food sources, animals, plants and water, and, of course for most, within the vast array of organics surrounding the wild animal. It is here, in these 'organics', that I feel we have fallen short, walking away from natural Bio-Activity in a safe and measured way, removing a ready source of supply of certain B vitamins and, of course, the array of full-spectrum minerals, amino acids and the rest of the microbiota.

The earth itself is a potent, sustaining and nurturing force. We can view this 'earth', whether that be soil, organic matter, mineral-rich water run-off or of course through gut-transference as a source of vital nutrition. If we remove normal developed access to these core processes, we then can cause a potential shortfall. As a further example of recent captive under provision, as opposed

> The earth itself is a potent, sustaining and nurturing force. We can view this 'earth', whether that be soil, organic matter, mineral-rich water run-off or of course through gut-transference as a source of vital nutrition."

to that of the wild, we can look at a readily available food source for many species all over the world. There are many species of reptile that will predate upon eggs in the wild (avian and reptilian). This 'many species' includes many species of snake and lizard. They consume these either by seeking out whole eggs or as opportunist feeding after finding and then consuming in part or as a whole source, broken eggs. A lack of supply in captivity therefore could cause over time a shortfall of many of the useful compounds including Biotin (B7). Shortages are noted as already stated with neurological and dermal 'dis-ease'. Care always should be taken, of course, but adding quail eggs into the full-spectrum and well-supplemented diet for many species, including the corn snake, may be greatly beneficial overall, especially for those animals that suffer with non-humidity related shedding issues. Again, the watchword here is 'full-spectrum' diet. One or two quail eggs every fortnight or even just 'in season' for some species could be viewed as being wholly beneficial, reversely providing a box each and every night would quickly cause a whole host of nutritional problems. It is all about balance and variety.

We also must take into account that the helpful bacteria living inside of the intestines can produce some of the group, including B12. This does not mean that they can make all that they need at all times; rather, this process itself is dependent on a full and varied diet, an active and healthy gut flora culture, wild levels of hydration and, of course, good general health to start with. The process is also affected by drug treatment, including the use of antibiotics and chemical parasite killers. We therefore must start to think of the knock-on effects that the use of any drug or change to the diet and some external parameters may have on our nutritional provision as a whole. If left unchecked, a reduction can be caused. In the case of a shortfall in B12, symptoms are shown as a reduction in the speed of normal growth and a loss of control over the limbs. As a group, I feel that amphibians are hit hard with this particular shortfall.

Certain other foods, including brassicas, contain inhibitors which, if overfed—that is, fed at a non-natural level or as a sole staple—will reduce the body's ability to assimilate and use members of the group. As always, variety of dietary provision is the key to success. Should we not feed proteins and brassicas to our green iguanas or tortoises? Of course we should feed them. On the whole, they are useful; in moderation is the key, however, and as part of a well though-out and mixed diet.

The group was originally thought of as just 'Vitamin B'; however, eventually, each modern member of the group was divided and split up, and then again re-classified into numerical order. As you will see, there are gaps in the numerical list of this group. Vitamins B 4, 8, 10 and 11 are now not classified as B-group vitamins but are thought of as separate agents or amino acids. This once again does not make them of any less importance; rather, we must think of nutrition as being all-encompassing and as being as widely broad spectrum as possible. Just as we would never even consider not using a good quality calcium powder, similarly, we should never consider not using or providing for the rest of the elements of which the earth makes so plentiful to the animals that live in its ecosystems. This comment sounds flippant, even impossible, but I assure you that good full-spectrum feeding is a very simple process that just takes a little extra thought rather than dumping a few unheated and unfed locusts into an enclosure three times a week or emptying that bag of supermarket salad into a bowl once a day. You will be amazed just how quickly an animal can grow, form good colour and start to display wild communication when energised both internally and externally properly.

This is a very important group of natural, water soluble compounds that would be readily available in many ways to all wild reptiles and amphibians. They would be consumed as part of a varied regular diet and, as such, would be topped-up and maintained in an optimal way inside of the animals system every time that food or water is consumed.

In a similar way to a degree of Vitamin A deficiency, a deficiency of any single one component, cycle, or all, of the group can have catastrophic effects on a captive animal's overall health. This is like a biological game of balance, removing just one block can cause other core processes and indicators to fall away entirely or to become chronically unstable. Whatever happens, the animal has entered a period of nutritional instability and, as a whole, remains fragile. This shortfall would not only manifest itself in illness but also as a lack of physical and mental energy, even when properly heated. Symptoms and outworking's are commonplace with nervous disorders, including lethargy, aggression and tremors and is a key contributor to sexual dysfunction and a lack of successful reproduction, in both sexes. Over time, the blood would be affected and major organ dysfunction is also likely to go on to develop.

The good news is that life, as a whole, is a tough, unstoppable force. Levels of B vitamin deficiency, in my mind, are chronic (including with our own species), affecting in some way most of the animals we keep. The good news is that, just as with mammals, including our own species, this deficiency can be largely rectified quite quickly with the addition of the correct variety and potency of the group into the diet. Being water-soluble, they are easily assimilated, and the blood chemistry is quickly balanced. Even some very sick animals can find a level of therapeutic effect and some seem to go on to be totally cured. Some , in reverse, will have gone beyond the point of at home help. As such, the advice of a good reptile-focused vet should always be sought.

This group of vitamins is also found in live or dead animals when provided as food sources. Some of the members of this group can also be obtained directly from the earth, water, plants or even as stated as manufactured inside of the animal itself, with some of the group again found in uncooked, fertilised eggs. Vitamin B, as a group, is a vastly important and poorly understood group of compounds in reptiles. We can see that the animals themselves have a need for them and that their provision is wide-ranging in the wild. As such, we, as forward-thinking keepers, must start to place as much importance on this group as we do for vitamin D3, Ca and A.

Vitamin B1 (Thiamine):

Vitamin B1 is a water-soluble vitamin that does not build-up to toxic levels and which is not stored inside of the body. It should form part of the wild diet as part of regular feeding. Vitamin B1 is required in the production of hydrochloric acid. It is recognised as essential for blood health and circulation. It also plays a role in keeping blood circulation effective and in maintaining muscular development, eye health, effective digestion and the health of the nervous system. A lack of B1 in birds has been linked to the neurological conditions that cause 'stargazing', with this condition also impacting certain groups of reptile—especially some of the colour mutations. It is possible that a good source of B1 can reduce the occurrence of this condition. Vitamin B1 is found mainly in whole animals, legumes, fruits and beans, and also is found in fish, in which it can become problematic in terms of oversupply to fish-eaters, including the family of Garter snakes (*Thamnophis sp*). Importantly, it is most likely that reptiles would obtain this in the wild through insect gut flora and content, plant matter ingestion, and from the blood and internal organs of mammalian, reptilian and avian sources of food. High levels of folic acid are thought to inhibit the use and transition of B1 through the system and, as such, should be measured and balanced accordingly.

Vitamin B2 (Riboflavin):

Vitamin B2 is another water-soluble vitamin that is absorbed easily and which is known to play a very useful role in maintaining energy levels, blood production and organ development. Vitamin

B2 also is key in the reproduction of skin and scales, and is required in ensuring the balance of effective shedding and re-growth. A lack of this vitamin indeed could be a contributing factor with animals that do not shed properly or even those demonstrating an unexplained stunted growth. B2 is also required for egg-production and in the maintenance of sexual health, and thus the reproductive potency of reptiles. B2 also helps to keep the eyes healthy: in some cases, apparent eye disease has been linked to organ disease from a critical deficiency of this vitamin. Like most of the B vitamins, Vitamin B2 works and interacts with the others from the group, and is critical in the final use of Vitamin B6 and folic acid. It is found largely in the same food sources as vitamin B1. It is not thought that this vitamin can be critically oversupplied, although it does seem to have a limiting factor in terms of captive reptile care. B2 does seem to be broken down very quickly by ultraviolet; therefore, it may be prudent to directly feed food items supplemented with this vitamin and to not leave the food source in ultraviolet exposure for extended periods.

Vitamin B3 (Niacin):

Working with other vitamins from this group, Vitamin B3 supports red blood cell production and helps to maintain good circulation. It is another vitamin in the group that is key to aiding good digestion; in fact, a deficiency may initially present as a reduced appetite.

The vitamin is also key for maintaining a healthy nervous system. The vitamin also plays an important part in insulin synthesis and in the production and balancing of oestrogen and testosterone. This is another compound that aids skin production and therefore eases the shedding process. Vitamin B3 is found in the all of the same food sources as B1 and B2. It is most likely that it would be obtained from eating whole animals and eggs, as well as from legumes for herbivores. An oversupply of this vitamin has been linked to excessive itching, blood poisoning and foetal malformations in animal and human studies, although there do not seem to be any defined results in terms of a large oversupply to reptiles and amphibians.

Vitamin B5 (Pantothenic Acid):

Vitamin B5 is another water-soluble vitamin that is easy to absorb and does not have ready stores inside of the body. This vitamin must be replaced as part of a normal and balanced diet. As with others in the group, this vitamin works with and allows the proper use of amino acids, and is vital in maintaining skin and bone production. Vitamin B5 is also used as part of the digestion process. A lack of B5 is also linked to poor egg production and infertility. Vitamin B5 is also important in the cycle of production for vitamin D and, as such, we should seek to provide this in a balanced way. Vitamin B5 is not known to have a toxic level.

The vitamin is found in whole animal food sources and eggs, as well as legumes. It is not known whether omnivores obtain this vital element from eating plants or from the stomach content of the insects being consumed. It can also be found in honey and grains. In fact, the word *pantothenic* is derived from a Greek word meaning 'from everywhere'.

Vitamin B6 (Pyridoxine):
Similar to the others in this group, this is a water-soluble vitamin without the ability to be readily stored inside of the body. This is an important element that has a huge effect on the central nervous system if in short supply over a long period of time. B6 plays a vital role in the production of red blood cells, and is used in the digestion process by allowing the metabolism of fats, proteins and carbohydrates. Moreover, B6 also allows the effective production and use of hormones, and works with B3 in its role. B6, like most others in the group, is found in the blood, liver and the brain of whole animals and in B-rich vegetation. It is also found in fresh and fermented fruits and, as such, would be available to those species seeking out these fruits in the wild.

Vitamin B7 (Biotin):
Not much is known about this vitamin and its effects on reptiles. In most animals, it is produced internally in the gut as part of

normal digestion, although there is a chance of depletion to those on restricted diets and with other under lying diseases. B7 plays an important role in the synthesis of fatty acids and works with others in the group to provide energy and to aid amino acid assimilation. B7 is required for stable and healthy cell growth, as well as for the production of the fatty acids required for good digestion and assimilation. A critical lack has been linked to skin and hair complaints, and is also linked to certain bone disorders, such as certain forms of arthritis. This vitamin is found in eggs and in green leafy plants. It is not thought that an animal can be overdosed on this compound. As with many of the B group of vitamins, the use and assimilation of this compound can be affected badly during and shortly after antibiotic treatment. It therefore is wise to include a supplement during treatment.

Vitamin B9 (Folic Acid):
B9 is a very important member of this family of compounds. Not only does it work with the other members of the group, but it is very easy to become deficient through a restricted diet. A critical lack of folic acid will not allow good cell reproduction; as such, even minor cuts and infections can become very problematic in reptiles and amphibians. It is even possible that a critical lack over a long period could alter the repair of the animals DNA itself. Importantly, B9 works in the intestine to allow the

proper assimilation of nutrients, and plays a vital role in blood production, and hormone and nerve health. B9 is also well documented to play an important part in sexual reproduction and foetal health, with no evidence that this does not also apply for reptiles. B9 also plays an important role in maintaining good brain function and a good hormonal balance. B9 would be found in whole animal food sources and in some broad green leafy plants, with moderate amounts also found in fruits and grains. One limiting factor is that cabbage and most of the brassicas seem to reduce the assimilation levels of folic acid. It is also thought that Vitamin C aids with metabolising folic acid. If the animal in question is fed a mixed diet of these leafy sources that are so good for other compounds in the group, it may be beneficial to use a B9 supplement to increase the active levels of folates in the animal. It would seem that this vitamin does play an important part in the life of a reptile and should be provided to a captive subject as part of a balanced diet. Notably, B9 can and probably should be fed to insects as part of a measured gut-loading process, which means it can then be passed onto the predator in a natural way.

Vitamin B12 (Cobalamin and Cyanocobalamin):

Vitamin B12, as with the rest of the group, is a water-soluble vitamin but has a major difference in that it is able to be stored in small amounts inside of the liver and kidneys. Vitamin B12 is only required in very small doses, but these doses are extremely important to life. Vitamin B12 plays an active and essential role in red blood cell production and blood health, and is used in bone marrow production. It works alongside many other vitamins not only in the B group but also with Vitamin A and Vitamin C. This, in turn, affects the production, regulation and further use of the D vitamin group, and finally, along with Ca and P, allows good use and storage.

Vitamin B12 is also used to aid digestion and to promote healthy gut flora, and provides an important protective sheath over nerve endings (nerve cell insulators). A critical undersupply would result in core blood chemistry changes, which, in turn, would firstly affect energy levels and the ability to digest food adequately. If left untreated or undersupplied, this form of Hypovitaminosis B12 could lead to permanent blood and bone issues, as well as raising the risk of unrepairable neurological diseases.

Vitamin B12 is only really found inside of animals' intestines and livers, meaning that it can be provided for well as a part of a varied, well-fed (gutloaded) diet for live food-eaters. Live foods should be well pre-fed and hydrated before being offered up the food chain, whilst defrosted frozen mammals, birds and when pertinent, fish, as always, should originate from a well-fed and trusted source. Vitamin B12 has a reduced level of potency after cooking in terms of human diets.

Vitamin B12 is not, however, found inside of plants, which begs the question of how the herbivores obtain this essential vitamin. B12 is produced by microorganisms living inside of, or on the bodies of live prey sources or on decaying meat and fish. The organisms are not able to grow well on and definitely not inside of fruit or vegetation, but there is a possible answer to this question. Plants that are grown organically are found to have upon themselves some useable levels of B12. This is primarily from the manure-based soils in which they are grown. The bacteria responsible for B12 fares very well in faeces. It is entirely probable that B12 is ingested by herbivores simply by eating plants and fruits that have grown in a natural surrounding and that would be exposed to the dung of other animals.

They could also directly obtain this vitamin through the earth itself as they ingest mouthfuls of food, or otherwise from the practise of eating their own dung or that from the same species. It would seem that an overly sterile source of plant-based foods would not be ideal in captivity for herbivores long-term. It would of course seem sensible to grow our own feeder plants ourselves in a way that we can be sure of no chemical or insecticidal contamination.

These can then be fed to this group with the assurance of dietary provision. Sources of B12 in nature are whole animal prey items, notably mammal, reptile, avian or insects, and also can be found in fish and shell fish and also inside of the yolks of eggs. Moreover, it is safe to assume that small particles of B12 can be found and used on the outside of wild or organically grown plants. This also could be increased further by feeding the root network of the plant. B12 may be supplemented synthetically and should form part of a balanced full-spectrum supplement. Similarly, many whole reptile diets will have this vitamin added.

Related or historical members:
B4 (Choline): Referred to as choline, adenine or carnitine, B4 is added to many whole reptile diets and supplements. There are no records of death caused by deficiency of this compound alone but it does occur naturally in many plants, fruits, insects (via the consumption of plants) and of course whole animal sources. It is important for maintaining vital organ health (especially liver and kidneys), being one of the building blocks of life, enabling good cell health and neural communication. Its inclusion in a balanced way would therefore seem sensible.

B8 (Myo-Inositol): Seems to be produced through the conversion of sugars and amino acids in the intestines. It also seems to play a positive role in the oxygenation of haemoglobin.

B10 (Para-aminobenzoic acid): Used in human medicine to treat chronic skin and neurological conditions. Some animal studies also show a link to this compound and an increased level of protection against skin cancers occurring from UV damage. As such we may need to think more closely in time about its effects upon the level of dermal protection that a species has developed against the sun and the compounds action with this. It is produced inside of the body. It is found in whole grains, fungi and whole animal prey sources also.

Bioactivity and its Action against MBD and other Nutritional Diseases

There is a vitally important point to be made here: Bio-Activity does not cause nor does it cure MBD, or any of the other hundreds of potential nutritional and environmental complaints. It is entirely possible that you could maintain a live culture that was visibly fizzing with a whole host of beneficial custodians and is teaming with positive microbial life, where the plants were growing out of the doors and where humidity is maintained well but that the animals still presented with fatal levels of nutritional disease. Simply changing from newspaper to soil will not stop these worrying and avoidable diseases.

Bio-Activity in and of itself is not a cure-all nor is it a magic bullet. It is not the answer to all of our historical herpetological woes and it never can be. It is, of course, within the theory of 'Wild

Re-Creation'™ through Bio-Activity that the fabled 'magic bullet' is hiding. Simply having a live substrate will not stop an under-provision of calcium. (See the next chapter for more on the D3 cycle and Ca.) Yes, it is this dedication to replicating the exact wild parameters of the species that we keep as closely as technology allows that Bio-Activity really starts to come into its own and can really start to help us to provide for and to help to protect our animals going forward.

So, yes, in a real sense, Wild Re-Creation™ through Bio-Activity is a vital tool that can be used to help to protect our animals against and can offer some kind of relief from historic mineral deficiency, but are there any other uses?

The answer to this is yes, but the total beneficial effects of this theory upon our animals could be almost impossible to quantify as true Wild Re-Creation™ through Bio-Activity can affect every single part of biology right from the microscopic symbiosis of microbes and the animals themselves right up to the health of the organs and skin. We must not direct our minds away from the fact that this system should impact the animals that we keep in ways that we currently simply do not yet understand. I have tried to demonstrate the varied feeding processes of live animals. If we can grasp the interactions of these processes, we soon will start to see how the 'environment' itself has a positive and long-term interaction with our animals.

There is calcium everywhere—in plants, animals and in water. It is also abundant in the soil. A wild animal will be ingesting calcium and the whole broad spectrum of earth minerals pretty much every time it opens its mouth. This is an unrelenting and constant form of essential mineral and microbial supply. We then wonder why, when we feed our pet reptiles a few times a week with un-dose-able powders that tend to fall off of the foods before ingestion, why they still display signs of deficiency. We call or label these many varied nutritional deficiencies MBD.

The animals, in all truth, are simply not getting enough of these natural, earth-bound elements, nor are they supplied in the right ratios or in a broad enough spectrum to mimic the animal's wild evolved processes. Speak to any reptile-focused vet and they will tell you that MBD, in all its forms, are recognised in the clinic pretty much every day; this is an indication that we still have much to learn and many essential processes to change and adapt to.

Calcium is very bio-available and very easy to obtain. It is everywhere and is found in pretty much everything, but it is in and of itself only one element. We, as keepers, tend to coat the food items that we offer our pets with calcium powders and with very good intention (this is required but maybe more useable and more effective to long-term health and wellbeing when made part of a full-spectrum, natural mineral provision). But what about the rest of the minerals found in the earth? What about the interactions they must have with each other during and after ingestion, in addition to as part of the assimilation, storage and use process? We, as keepers, must start to think of mineral provision as an all-encompassing, full-spectrum process. If an animal has to ingest 40+ minerals with every few grains of dirt that enter the mouth or every time they drink in the wild, then there is a use and an interaction for them in captivity. In reality, the provision of the rest of the earth-bound minerals are just as important, if not more important, to the mineralisation process than many of us have ever realised. Providing for a full-spectrum of the elements in the correct way and in the correct quantities, and in many different formats, will help us to further increase the efficacy of our systems than the usual dust and dump method of simply providing plain calcium ($CaCO_3$).

> A well-fed and well-maintained, properly functioning Bio-Active system will be able to help you to provide these earth-bound minerals at all times and in a way that is natural for the animal to obtain them."

Again, look to wild adaptation, look to the many evolved processes, and you soon will see that mineral supply is a constant thing and does not just occur every third day as if by magic, spontaneously coating the food they find. Then remember that, in the wild—and even with all of this incidental provision—wild animals still need to self-supplement. We do not currently, as keepers, place a high enough importance on mineral, natural vitamin and microbial provision. We still, on the whole, rely upon branded powders alone and we administer these in a 'dust and dump' fashion with no real dosing or guidance per species or per gram of body weight. Bio-Activity, on the other hand, can help us to provide a wider variety of minerals, vitamins and microbes in a way that is closer to the methods of natural ingestion in the wild. A well-fed and well-maintained, properly functioning Bio-Active system will be able to help you to provide these earth-bound minerals at all times and in a way that is natural for the animal to obtain them.

"A well fed Steppe runner benefiting from a deep substrate in which to dig"

How is that? An organic and live, well-designed substrate will not only be safe to use and to ingest but also will contain a broad spectrum of minerals and vitamins and, as such, form part of the Wild re-created diet. The animal will be able to obtain more of these elements very easily and with the addition of vitamins such as D3 from the natural source, whether assimilated, stored or used well. As such, yes, Wild Re-Creation,™ through Bio-Activity, is an important tool in the ongoing fight against MDB in all of its potentially murderous forms.

The inclusion of volcanic-based soil re-vitalisers will help to supply essential minerals for the plants. They also will remain available and potent for the animals to ingest as part of the normal feeding process. We also must once again remind ourselves, as forward-thinking keepers, of the great importance of adequate hydration. We can become fixated on good mineral and vitamin supply and dietary variety, but without the proper provision of water and humidity per species, all of these processes will be hindered in some way. Dietary variety, water, solar energy (heat and UV), vitamin and mineral provision, enrichment and interaction all should be viewed with the same level of importance.

The importance of D3 and Ca—A Short Reminder including Brumation

(For an in-depth look at this subject, please see 'The Arcadia Guide to MBD and its Elimination in Captivity' and 'The Arcadia Guide to Reptile and Amphibian Nutrition' by the same author.)

The relationship between Vitamin D3 and Ca and P is well-known and has been extensively documented in both human and animal medicine. We ourselves, as a species, are on the cusp of a D3 deficiency crisis with core 'news' and medical papers and reports now suggesting a resurgence of avoidable diseases, such as rickets. We have, as a generation, walked away from our own 'wild' needs as we seek to protect ourselves from the power of the sun (that is, that we have become potentially negatively affected due to climate change and damage from the ozone layer) and to reduce the risk and incidence of skin cancers. The flip side, of course, is that we do not obtain enough dietary D3 on the whole and, as such, are, on the whole, deficient. Who knows how far this reduction will go or just how badly affected we will be over a long period of time, and what knock-on diseases will affect our own generation and those to follow. One thing is for sure, however: our own requirements, just like those of the captive reptile, have not changed and will not do so. As such, these apparent and now long-term undersupplies become more of a direct and fundamental 'fact' rather than a theoretical 'risk'.

Without access to usable D3 in the quantities that a particular species has evolved to utilise, it could be suggested that a species would not be able to assimilate, store and/or use Ca and P in its own body to the upper—and, as such, wild—levels. I believe that light and energy from light has many more interactions within a reptile's body, and that these interactions and uses must not be simply glossed over. As with all aspects of nature, everything must work together in unison to build and to sustain a healthy animal that, at its core, has the need to project its genes into the future in a sustainable way without risk to itself or its offspring.

The importance of Ca; Ca is required in most aspects of reptile health and wellbeing. The D3 cycle and the importance of Ca supplementation does not just refer to bone health alone. Ca, for instance, is vitally important to the health and function of the vital organs and further controls a muscle's ability to contract effectively (a lack of Ca poses just a serious risk to the health of the heart as it does to the bones). Ca also plays a vital role in maintaining good neurological health amongst many other biological uses.

"Plated Lizards are almost never bred in captivity. With the advent of better systems this should become a thing of the past."

> Deficiency of Ca is the primary reason that many captive reptiles have presented with MBD (metabolic bone disease) over the years."

If the levels of Ca available are reduced to a critical level, an animal could experience organ malfunction and, if no measured correction is applied, death may occur. This deficiency of Ca is the primary reason that many captive reptiles have presented with MBD (metabolic bone disease) over the years. If a species does not have access to the correct levels of Ca or does not have the ability to assimilate and store this Ca, then it then may use a wild survival technique to release Ca back into the bloodstream. We can use another wild survival method to demonstrate this in principle. Seasonal brumation allows a species to survive without permanent physical detriment during the colder seasons. In this time of reduced feeding and activity in the wild, the animal will go through a seasonal period of lack. This lack of food and energy from light in the form of I-R (heat) and a drop in the terrestrial UVI could lead to a situation where an animal's reserves of Ca become overly depleted. In turn, this could lead to organ function issues and, as such, I believe that the wild animal has a self-preservation technique. We call this brumation.

I myself believe that brumation also can be enacted due to a lowering of the air pressure in the area in which the animal is kept. This explains why many animals have a tendency to demonstrate reduced levels of activity and feeding in the winter months, even when the captive temps are maintained to the upper quantity. I feel that it is the same metrological changes that cause localised brumation that also start the local 'wild indigenous' brumations, hibernations and, of course, migrations in these wild populations.

A change in barometric pressure and the magnetic fields surrounding the earth are now thought to be important factors in this. There is still much to do to prove this but, for me, in 2016, I am happy to subscribe to this thinking. It simply makes sense, both at a biological and at an evolutionary level. If we factor in 'survival of the fittest', then we can see a clear and positive use for processes such as brumation and hibernation, not only for the long-term survival of a species but so that the next generation is able to get the very best start from the passed on 'stores' of both the mother and father animals.

But how does brumation protect an animal through these wild seasonal changes and how does a potential depletion occur? Brumation protects an animal as its levels of activity will reduce. This places a lower load on the animal's body as it starts to live from the stores of fat and minerals that have been obtained during times of plenty. Ca, as an example, will be continuously supplied to the body to ensure that organ function and muscle contraction continues. In very simple terms, the brain will ask the blood to release stored Ca (and other minerals) from the bones with the aim of maintaining positive vital organ function. In the wild, this process is very safe indeed as spring and summer will arrive once again and the animal, therefore, will be able to obtain and use the increased levels of surrounding solar energy and food, and then re-balance or re-stock the stored minerals within its own system with no lasting harm to its own body. We go from the historical captive system of 'boom and bust' to 'boom and effective supply from plentiful stores followed by boom again' in a constant and effective cyclical fashion.

In a captive situation where energy from light is not provided to the wild level or in a way that is suitable/usable to an individual species, 'spring and summer' never actually seems to arrive and the incessant slow depletion of the skeletal reserves continues day after day. After a period of time, sometimes quite short in reality, the bones can become so depleted of minerals that they may even start to twist and break. Other symptoms affecting reptiles with MBD can include both organ malfunction and neurological issues, both of which are quite common. Long-term

"Royal pythons can be tricky to feed in the winter season"

and untreated MBD can finalise as early death, either naturally or via human intervention.

Of course, D3 can be provided for in the diet for some species; this would be part of Wild Re-Creation™ in those animals that eat whole animal or fish items, but what about the herbivores and those that consume almost entirely a sole insect diet? What about the serious risk of an over- or under-supply of dietary D3 and its long-term effects on animals? And what about the issues surrounding the provision of a correct dose and its effective delivery? I can think of very few species of animal that have no interaction with the sun at all. As such, we can be rest assured that our provision of Ca is able to be utilised if we rely upon a UV system that re-creates the wild need of the species in question. Then, dietary D3 can be used in whole animal food sources and/ or as a synthetic compound in greatly reduced amounts to help to 'top-up' stored levels as required, thus providing well for any given species. I cover this subject in greater detail in 'The Arcadia Guide to Reptile and Amphibian Nutrition'.

As we have seen, calcium is essential to life. It is a potent building block that is widely available through food and water, as well as through the normal living processes in the wild environment. It is with our suggested system of Wild Re-Creation™ that I believe that we can be sure of an effective supply of the full-spectrum of earth-bound vitamins and minerals, and the ongoing biological use of these vital elements.

THE D3 CYCLE

www.arcadia-reptile.com/the-d3-cycle

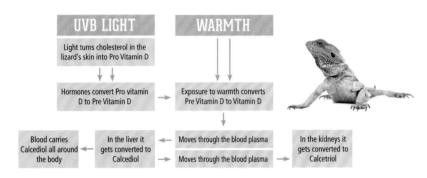

The D3 Cycle is a chemical and hormonal change in the body of an animal, which goes on to produce vitamin D3. This is a biological process that is dependent on many external factors including access to natural light, heat, cool and rest. It is worth noting that although vital to the well being of reptiles, UV exposure plays many more roles in the body than just the D3 cycle. Impacts on sight, breeding and mental well being are all documented and are undergoing continued research.

This amazing process begins when a cholesterol called pro vitamin D(7DHC) is produced in the animal's skin (it is a natural process in humans too). When this cholesterol is exposed to natural light (including light in the UVB wavelength (290-315nm)), this cholesterol is turned in the skin membrane into pre vitamin D.

After exposure to warmth, this newly manufactured pre vitamin D is converted (in the skin membrane) into vitamin D3. It is essential to have this heating up period alongside UV radiation. Vitamin D3 is then sent out into the blood plasma and is bound with a vitamin D binding protein. This is then carried to the liver where this part of this vitamin is converted to a hormone called calcediol (25-hydroxy vitamin D3).

The blood carries this calcediol all around the body and into the kidneys where some of the hormone is turned into another hormone, called calcetriol. This compound then plays an essential role in calcium metabolism and controls the levels of calcium in the blood. Calcetriol also plays a huge role in the immune system and the cardiovascular system. It has been shown to lower the risk of cancers in the body and skin.

So we can see that exposure to natural sunlight is only the start of this amazing ability in reptiles and humans alike, to turn sunlight into life saving vitamins. This D3 cycle is dependent on the completion of the D3 cycle. If part of the cycle is missed out then the cycle cannot be completed properly. Changes and reactions would also be unable to be completed properly. This would result in an under provision of essential vitamins and hormones, and if supplementation were not used, a calcium crash could happen.

© **John Courteney-Smith, Arcadia Reptile.**

Taken from "GUIDE TO MBD AND ITS ELIMINATION IN CAPTIVITY."

Feeding, Enrichment and Obesity in Captive Animals

One of the areas in which many of us fail is truly understanding, myself included, and also failing to exactly provide for, the environmental enrichment and exercise of both the mind and body. Yes, just as with humans, many reptiles can suffer with obesity and the myriad of knock-on diseases that follow in its destructive wake. As such, reptiles need adequate space to move around properly; this is a form of exercise. They also need good mental stimulation. We refer to such a provision as enrichment.

So many of the modern 'whole food' products are packed full of empty base sugars and unsuitable fats and proteins, which our causing our animals to become overweight or even obese. Being fat or appearing 'well fed', however, is not an indicator to adequate or full-spectrum dietary provision. Rather, these animals are still able to suffer from chronic nutritional deficiencies.

An animal can easily be fed excessively and put on large volumes of weight and still suffer with a fatal shortage of Ca. In fact, I have seen many more than just one Bosc monitor that has become so fat that they can no longer walk properly, let alone climb or run. On top of this, they tend to display visible symptoms of serious calcium imbalance—this from a species that has developed over millennia to become a super lean, aggressive and fast reptile in the wild. Imagine the stress to the animal's biology and the long-term effect on its internal organs. We also must remember that, just because an animal looks well-fed or fat, it doesn't mean that it is actually 'well-fed' in terms of nutritional and mineral supply. Many of these animals can be termed as 'overfed' but remain in certain nutritional sectors 'starving to death' or under-provided for. Yes, I will state it again as this is an important point: an animal can be fat and still develop potentially fatal MBD.

It can also be said that 'empty' or nutritionally devoid (unbalanced or unnatural) foods cause obesity! Combine this with a lack of wild-like enrichment and poor provision for exercise and you have nothing more than a recipe for disease. A water dragon, for example, should be a lean and fast animal that can run, swim and leap from branch to branch. They should not be able to be picked up at will or have a girth twice as wide as the shoulders. They will, if allowed to, however, live a sedentary life and become very

"Blue Tongue Skink"

lazy in terms of finding their own food. The worst mistake many of us make is starting to hand-feed our animals. Reptiles are and will always be opportunist feeders. They can wait for very long periods of time and then grab hold of food as it passes by. In times of plenty, this is easy and safer than allowing full exposure by chasing through the forest or scrubland as they can tuck themselves away in the safety of their eco-system and wait

> Predator avoidance alone can cause an arboreal species to travel by land or by water for great distances indeed. This is exercise and stimulation."

for food to arrive. They still will need to hunt and move around, of course, as the localised wild environment is subject to a constant level change, risks and stresses, as well as changing seasons. Predator avoidance alone can cause an arboreal species to travel by land or by water for great distances indeed. This is exercise and stimulation.

By regular or obsessive target- or hand-feeding, the captive animal soon learns that everyday food will 'walk past', and all it has to do is to grab it and swallow. The need to expose oneself to the perceived localised dangers is reduced, and they will continue to wait unmoving, knowing that food will 'walk by' eventually. In reality, the process of them finding food, hunting it down and using the whole enclosure is just as important to the feeding process as the provision of food itself. We need to get their blood pumping, their muscles flexing and contracting, and their brains working. Remember: nutrition starts from the ground up and encompasses every part of an ecosystem.

In my mind, the well though-out provision of safe and measured lean times for healthy captive animals is just as important as the provision of times of plenty. Fats are naturally stored as winter reserves to be used as shown in the brumation chapter. If they are not used and enrichment is not catered to properly, the animal will become fat as the desire and inbuilt need to lay down fats for harder times will propel the animal to feed constantly. I once saw an 'old school' keeper feed almost 40 adult locusts to a Bosc monitor. He was under the impression that the animal was hungry and that this was its need; in reality, however, the animal was

"A young Bosc or Savanna Monitor showing good colour"

simply subject to a wild survival mechanism—one that dictates that it feeds as often as it can in the times of plenty so that the times of lack do not become a problem. The animal will feed and feed, but does this mean that it is good for it to do so?

Just because an animal feeds voraciously, it does not necessarily mean that it is well as a whole. Overfeeding and, in some cases, hand-feeding, simply places a strain on the animal, and a cycle of laziness begins that is very difficult to break.

Remember: a bearded dragon should be lean, fit, almost muscular and fast. It should not be lazing around sitting on the arm of the armchair apparently watching TV, nor should it be so fat that it is disinclined to climb when placed inside of its enclosure. This is a problem all of its own in its own right. If an animal has to alter its position to increase its ability to find heat and UVB energy but is so fat it cannot move or is disinclined to do so, then the animal will never reach the full physical energy levels required and, once again, will run the risk of a critical lack of minerals.

Exercise is a vital part of Wild Re-Creation™ for captive animals. As such, we should make sure that our enclosures are big enough to allow the full and free movement of your intended species. We should make sure that our decoration provides both physical and mental stimulation, and we must make sure that we do allow an animals system to fully digest and make use of the foods we feed them before stuffing them full of food again and again. Lizards should be able to run as they do in the wild and snakes should be able to climb. Frogs should be able to perch and spiders construct webs. In some small but important way, these species-specific practises are part of their core development and must be thoughtfully catered to. This, of course, is part of the keeping process and has both a use and an interaction in terms of external and internal health.

"Toad headed Agamas are both rare and require very large enclosures, this is key to their enrichment"

> We commonly now see zoo keepers hide food sources around the enclosures of larger lizards with the aim of allowing the animal to display more natural behaviour and to obtain physical exercise."

We also must factor into our enclosure design mental stimulation. Reptiles, I feel, on the whole, are far more sentient that we have historically afforded them. They are alert and able to use their minds to find food, water, safety and, of course, a mate. In my mind, providing good mental stimulation through high, wild-like light levels or intensities, adequate running or climbing space, and simply allowing a species to find or acquire food rather than being fed, is vitally important. We commonly now see zoo keepers hide food sources around the enclosures of larger lizards with the aim of allowing the animal to display more natural behaviour and to obtain physical exercise. I feel that this does indeed have a positive effect on overall reptilian mental wellbeing. In time, science will, I am sure, allow us to prove the benefits one way or the other.

"A large Mellor's chameleon, historically almost impossible to keep. They certainly require a huge enclosure, peace and quiet and a full system of Wild Re-Creation"

The Leopard Gecko–

A Study into the Evolving Captive Care and Attitudes to One of the World's most Frequently Kept Species

[Two examples of species' care, as an example to the 'theory', as originally printed in 'Practical Reptile Keeping' Magazine, as an edited source, follow.]

The Leopard Gecko is a ground-dwelling species that originates from the arid scrublands of Afghanistan and Pakistan. It has been kept for over three decades by pretty much every sector of society. This vast base of keepers have not only been able to farm this as a captive-bred species, but they have been able to alter its genes through selective breeding for both colour and size. This has led to hundreds of colour variants, and propelled the species further into society than most other 'pet' species of reptile could ever achieve. But there have been problems along the way: mot only do some of these genetic changes have knock-on biological and neurological- effects upon the animal, but the current mass-keeping practices are far removed from the wild evolved needs of the species.

A great deal of poor information has been passed on from breeder to breeder over the years; one such example is that the Leopard Gecko is a nocturnal species. We now know that the animal is far from being nocturnal in its wild range; rather, we refer to it as being crepuscular. A crepuscular animal is described as one that is more active at dawn and dusk rather than in the predator rich and hot core day time. The Leopard Gecko is quite crepuscular in the home range, but there are many reports of them being seem even in full daytime desert sunlight, openly basking, hunting and maintaining their territory.

We must keep in mind that this species originates from an area of the world with a huge amount of solar energy—Afghanistan, Pakistan. This level of solar energy indeed can be referred to as being similar to the Australian outback in the summer. Whatever way you look at it, the energy available from light, even in the evenings, is far greater than the level currently available in Northern Europe, even in the daytime in the summer. Whichever way you look at things, evolution has allowed these groups of animals to obtain everything that they need from their environment in the safest possible way.

They have evolved a very thin and light penetrating skin with wide black spots to help draw in heat quickly. This is an evolved mechanism common to nocturnes and crepuscular species all over the world. It allows them to utilise solar energy, whether that be as infra-red (heat) or indeed all of the other terrestrial wavelengths, very quickly and very efficiently, with minimum risk to the animal

"This is an example of a re-created terrain typical of the leopard gecko"

and with the greatest results. This, once again, is core evolution in action, predator-avoidance and taking everything that you need from your local environment to allow oneself to thrive and project one's genes into future generations with minimum risk to oneself.

We know that Leopard Geckos are largely insect-eaters in the wild, and here's the point: insects and plants do not contain or deliver Vitamin D3 but rather D2, which has no action on the sustained calcium cycle. Remember: if there is a lack of D3, there always will be a lack of available Ca to utilise in and around the bones. To obtain D3 naturally, you will need to eat whole animal sources or have direct exposure to sunlight. Yes, Leos will gladly eat mice and chicks and the lke, but this would make up a very small part of the wild diet and be very seasonal. With a lack of manmade chemicals in the wild, they also will have had to have become totally solar-reliant or would suffer as a species.

Some keepers ask for proof that there indeed is a solar interaction in crepuscular species. This is fairly basic and easy to achieve now; we can see from simple D3 serum level blood testing that there is indeed a solar interaction after exposure to UVB and that the D3 cycle is fully active in the species, as it is with almost every other. We also must realise that one cannot suggest that a species will use one wavelength of solar energy without being exposed to the rest as sunlight is very much terrestrially 'full-spectrum'. In short, it would, I think, make a mockery of the whole theory of evolution by natural selection to suggest that an ectotherm would use infra- red (heat) for the energy that it needs to move and to feed and that it would use UVA to see the world via tetrachromacy and to then suggest that they evolved away from having a need for manufacturing its own D3, which is started by being exposed to UVB—UVB being one of the biggest free sources of solar energy around our world. It just makes no evolutionary sense.

"Leopard gecko basking, Daniel Courteney-Smith"

We must also accept that light does not just travel in straight lines from the sky downwards and then, as if by magic, simply disappear. No, light travels in million/billions of angles and reflects and refracts off of anything and everything. This is how light and energy from light can reflect off the ground and enter caves, tunnels and rock networks. Reflected sun is pretty much just as active as direct sunlight. (See the increased risk of sunburn to humans when in or near water in the sun or indeed even when surrounded by snow.) What a cool predator-avoidance skill it is to be able to hide in between the rocks and scrubland and in tunnel entrances, nooks and crannies, and still be able to energise one's body properly; that is nature at its finest and it is simply awe-inspiring.

Sunlight is full-spectrum and active. Even in low light levels, there can be quite high indexes or quantities of UVB energy. As a rule of thumb, if you can see your hand 4" in front of your face, you will be able to quantify and measure an active or potent level of UVB energy in the wild. We also have to acknowledge that the world has differing weather zones. The solar index of the UK in summer averages at around 5-6 at midday, whilst the Afghan desert can mimic this level of energy much earlier and later on in the day. In reality, the index to which we are exposed in the UK in summer is like their early morning or dusk period.

We have to look at the whole environment surrounding the species; we then can see how it obtains water, what food sources it commonly takes, exactly the ratio of natural earth minerals around the burrows and in the wild water courses, and the number and species of plants growing close by. This, in itself, is important as it can hold a clue to the amino and mineral provision by the inverts that consume the plants to the gecko that consumes the insect. You see, if we can open our minds to wild replication, we can come to understand how 'that' can have a positive impact upon our pets in both health, enrichment and of course our level of enjoyment.

Can Leos be kept in a warm box with no light and be expected to reproduce? 100% yes, they can, and they have been bred this way for many years. Does this practice fulfil their wild and core-evolved needs without a chance of long-term risk and, as such, protect them from potential generational harm and, in essence, allow them to 'thrive' as they have evolved to do so? I cannot see that it can. The ability to reproduce successfully is simply no indication of levels of overall health. The fact that many species, including our own, will reproduce in less than favourable surroundings is simply testament to the fact that the natural desire to project one's genes into the future is a far stronger force than the current or even future environmental limitations.

We also have to accept that, although vitamin powders indeed are totally essential to the practice of keeping exotics, they are far from perfect. Fat soluble vitamins, including A, D and E, are all potentially toxic if over- or under-supplied. Some say that an oversupply is simply not possible with current products; I simply cannot accept that this is actually the case. An over-provision of D3 in the diet will lead not only to fatty liver issues but also hypercalcemia, which, in itself, is potentially fatal, mimicking an under-provision and leading to coronary heart disease, etc. An under-provision, over time, will lead to the depletion of available bone stores of Ca and can lead to hypocalcaemia and metabolic bone disease. The fact that vets still see so much MBD is cause enough to think that we still have much to learn.

> Vitamin A can be safely and effectively provided for via a similar natural cycle by feeding foods rich in natural carotenoids. "

The worrying issue, as already stated, is that no one seems to know how to accurately dose an animal with synthetics alone. It is worrying that we do not know how much powder or oil is required per species and per gram of body weight, sex and season, not to mention the lack of access to an accurate dose delivery mechanism. In my mind, this places the keeper on a knife's edge of a potential over- or under-provision. The issue, of course, is that dietary D3, when over-provided for, is stored by the body, which is the same for Vitamin A. If D3 is provided for via solar radiation, the body will 'self-regulate' itself to its own core need at that time. The same can be said for Vitamin A: if obtained via carotenoids, there seems to be no risk of over-production. The over-supply of D3, therefore, cannot be an issue as it is if supplied via the mouth if the index or quantity of UVB provided matches the wild and as per the light and shade method, which, in itself, allows good self-regulation.

Vitamin A can be safely and effectively provided for via a similar natural cycle by feeding foods rich in natural carotenoids. Again, the body only makes what it needs as it needs it and dumps the rest, unlike with a pure source, where storage and over supply remain as a risk.

B-group vitamins and minerals are largely water-soluble and wash through the body, even if over-provided. Largely, they can be referred to as non-toxic and can and should be fed frequently. This, in itself, replicates the ingestion of the animal's surroundings. Reptiles are supposed to eat dirt; it provides them with the many natural earth-bound vitamins, minerals and trace elements. In captivity, where we have a reduced availability of natural products, using good supplements simply makes up for the shortfall.

Are there any limitations to wild re-creation for this species and are there any real differences in keeping mutations to the original wild cousin? Of course, there must be: we have altered through selective breeding what nature allowed to develop and, in some cases, there will be knock-on effects.

One worrying limitation, of course, is the perpetuation of the red-eyed colour variants that have become very sensitive to light (all light). We must, however, make sure that we keep in mind that the core biological processes of the animal are just the same as they are with the wild variant: they have the same processes and needs as the wild animal but may have a limited way of obtaining them.

The issue with eye health is worrying: man has selectively bred the species for colour variants, which has moved the animal away from its wild, evolved and natural state. What has happened is that we have bred a group of animals, no matter how attractive and wondrous, away from being a highly evolved desert species and into—in the case of the enigma—being light-phobic. In reality, as stated, the animals still have the same natural evolved needs, but we have allowed a limitation to the provision of that need in the search for colour.

Care must be taken: common feedback is that albinos still openly bask in actually quite high indexes, but choose to shade the head whilst so doing. Evolution in action! Watch them change as they learn to take all that they need to, to thrive in the enclosure.

We also have to be careful with some morphs as the skin thickness and/or levels of protective melanin may have been reduced. Skin thickness represents a level of protection against the sun and a level of use for it. If we provide an index or quantity of solar energy to any and ALL species that is above the level of evolved protection, we then overdose the animal and risk dermal burns, cancers, etc. It is the same with humans and every other species: if we match the wild in a safe, measured and regulated way, we then will be some way to providing for our pets without risk or detriment. I would suggest that a background index of 1–3 and, as part of the light and shade method, is right for wild colour animals in captivity. A total of 0.50-1.00 could be provided for red-eyed variants whilst providing extra caves and using timers to provide defined illuminated periods.

For many years, hundreds of thousands of these animals have been produced without any access to sunlight via the addition of synthetic supplements into the diet. It is plain to everybody to see that this can be achieved well, but should this still be the case knowing what we now know? Does the wild need of a species and the fulfilment of its core-evolved biological processes need to be taken into mind, utilised and advised upon? In my mind—and from my own research—the answer is an emphatic yes. Making small changes now can reduce the risk of disease, increase productive lifespan, and help to breed better mineralisation back into further generations.

This will be an issue that causes arguments for a long time to come, yet old habits and thought processes die hard as it were. There is a definite 'we have done it this way for decades and everything is fine' and 'we must provide the best for our species and mimic the wild in doing so' split in the hobby which can actually become quite militant in some sectors.

We still have, and always will have, MUCH to learn: we are finding new things out all of the time and the industry will continue to change and adapt to cater to the welfare of all species in an effective and ethical manor. This will mean even better young and happy, healthier, stronger animals with less chance of disease going forward.

Phelomedusa Sauvingii—

A Look into its Wild Habitat and the
Provision of Accurate Captive Care

Basically, as with every aspect of exotic animal care, we have to look to the actual evolved (core) needs of a species—per species and subspecies! We need to look intricately at the needs and actions of the species, including the actual everyday patterns of behaviour per season.

We have to look to the wild environment, the average weather patterns and seasonal cycles and, of course, the average solar index of the given locality per season and over as long a period of time as records allow. This is research gold to the exotic animal keeper.

We look at rainfall, the quantity and longevity of the rainy season or seasons. We look at wind factor and the given elevation above sea level per species (the higher a species is found the higher the available index will potentially be). We look the wild diet and the method of water ingestion. whether it is lapped directly from pools or obtained from rain rivulets running down a tree or from capillary action collected across the body or even from the simple opening of the mouth in the rain. We should also factor in the 'nutritional content' of wild water—it is far from 'pure'? No, it will contain Ca and many other minerals. This can and does play an active role in nutritional provision.

In short, we look at every aspect of the habits and environment of the wild species or subspecies, and make good notes. From these, we will see just how the seasons can affect a species. In the case of P sauvagii, we can see a direct link between the changing of the seasons of the rather harsh environments in which they live and their resting and breeding cycles.

We can see that they obtain a vast solar index in the wild and we can see how they have adapted to life in this rather hot, quite dry and windy place by evolving a level of protection against and a subsequent use for the sun. This, of course, comes from the waxy secretion that is wiped over the body. This does not just stop the frog from drying out, as was once thought, but also acts as a functioning sun block; however, this important evolutionary change is not an indication to the species' lack of solar requirement. Rather, this clever adaption has, in a similar way to the thick skins of arid lizard species, allowed the frog to take what it needs from the sun in the safest possible method. It really is a case of 'six and two threes': either you have a thin skin and develop a crepuscular tendency and pop out and energise quickly, or you have a thick skin and spend a much longer period of time in the sun or, in the case of this group, you develop the ability to use 'sunscreen'. The biological changes after exposure are still largely the same: these are just differing ways of obtaining the required dose of energy. Remember, just because an animal is found asleep by day does not mean that it has evolved to live in the dark. Just as a human burns when asleep in the sun, the core biological processes still plays out in terms of UVB to D3. You do not have to be awake to benefit in full from the energy of the sun.

So how do we implement this knowledge into our at home enclosures? Well, it really is very simple indeed. We use the knowledge that we have of the wild animal both proactively and sensibly. This is always our 'base' point. This is the place where we can start to build our technology around the animal in 'ITS' own enclosure as this, of course, is the actual evolved—and, as such, actual 'need'—of the species. For instance, if a species has evolved to thrive in full exposure under a solar index of 7-8 for 10 months of the year and at a thermal daily peak of say 34-36 and obtain hydration via mist and capillary action, then this is its biological need. Regardless, however we, as keepers, do this, it will always be their biological need and we must provide for it to be assured of its ability to truly thrive in captivity.

So, if we supplied that species with an index of 2-3 for 6 hours a day and ran the viv at 30 and left a bowl of water on the floor for it to drink from, we could not possibly be catering for its wild evolved biological needs. The animal would be in a real sense 'under-run' or under-provided for. This is where nutritional disease starts its long and chronic progression, whether this disease manifests from a lack of minerals—and, as such, poor organ and bone health—or a lack of water-soluble vitamins or even poor organ function from the lack of hydration. The clues to great captive care really are hidden in the wild.

Weather is rather fluid so we take averages and seek to set-up a system that is both proven safe and able to be accurately measured and maintained."

Reversely, this wild need will show the upper limits of the species' evolved solar protection method. As such, if we know that a species basks at an index of 5 and we provide 15, we will be over-providing for the species, pushing through the animal's solar protection, and thus risking, just as with humans, skin cancers and other biological problems. By over-providing, we do nothing other than put the animal at risk.

So, the next step is thorough research: get a plan down on paper so that you are happy with the actual needs of your chosen species as you see it. We have to take clues, of course; weather is rather fluid so we take averages and seek to set-up a system that is both proven safe and able to be accurately measured and maintained.

In the case of this highly evolved frog, we already know that they like it hot and dry for most of the year and have a regimented breeding cycle that is weather-specific. We can see that they are opportunistic feeders and will take food of many differing forms, all adding into their core nutritional provision over their lifespan (we should seek to mimic this also). We can see that temperatures are rather prone to change in the wild, but let's take an average of 28 degrees as a generally safe basking temp. This, of course, can be increased just before cycling right up to 34-36 depending on the locality of the frog to be kept. We can see that UV indexes for most of the year are shown as 'extreme', which means 9-11. However, we should not seek to irradiate the poor thing to this level in the confines of captivity. This is where a very fine line is drawn.

If 9-11 is the wild need, then surely we should provide 9-11 in captivity? Well, the answer, of course, is yes and also no. A frog in the wild has a vast space to move around and to find areas of strong sunshine as well as good gradients into shade. We also must remember that light—and, as such, UV—is not simply on or off, but has billions of gradients in-between, each one usable in an intricate way by the animal. Light reflects off of everything, meaning solar energy is made available in a myriad of graduations and angles. UV bouncing from a wet leaf or light stone and hitting the flanks and undersides of a species is just as important and active as the light that hits it back!

What about the frog's waxy secretion—does this indicate that the frog is protecting itself against the sun and therefore has no use for it? To this, we have to say an emphatic no. The level of protection against the sun is there so that the animal can bask safely and still be able to obtain essential solar energy and all of the biological processes that this causes. If we under-provide for this index, then the level of energy will not be able to penetrate through the secretion and go on to have the positive interaction that the frog has evolved to utilise. This is exactly the same for the green iguana, reticulated python or the bearded dragon—or indeed any other solar-reliant species. In the case of the green iguana, of course, they have evolved a need for and a level of protection against the sun via the thick almost armour-like skin. If the evolved total index is not provided for correctly, we cannot push through this level of protection, and there will be a potential shortfall in UVB exposure to D3 production (D3 cycle).

Okay, so we take an average: unless you have a room-sized enclosure for your frogs it will always be difficult to provide a safe graduation from the vast wild power into cool and shade. As such, we use an average and try our best to cause this usable sense of the wild in the enclosure size that we have. As we know, UVB is a weak wavelength that decreases in power as light travels forward. It is also impeded or even stopped entirely by plastics, glass and, of course, reduced in potency or index when travelling through a mesh. Therefore, we have to decide upon a basking

"Monkey Frog perched and basking"

index, match that with a basking area in the viv, and then choose a lamp that will provide for that index at that basking area or, in your case, 'perch'.

Of course, this has to be measurable. Therefore, we use a solarmeter of 6.5 to check the actual index and monitor this over the year. Let's say that, due to the level of protection against and the requirement for a specific index, coupled with daily activity patterns and/or course foliage cover, etc., that we should seek to provide an upper index basking zone of 5-6. This sounds about right to me. You therefore would choose a lamp that projects that index towards your basking area and then accordingly disperse that light round the area of projection by using broadleaf live plants and branches. We choose a lamp or lamps that are shorter than the viv and, as such, create 'light and shade' in which the frog can accurately self-regulate. We then sit back and watch: if the frog is constantly hiding after the settling in period and skulking about in the shadows, the index could be too high for its needs; reversely, if it is sitting up as high as it can right under the lamp, then move the perch up half an inch at a time until it stops reaching forward, but never exceed the 'safe' index—let's say 8.

As with all of these things, it is never a single simple answer that suits all' we can have a rough guess as to what is needed but we will also need tools to take measurements to become accurate with regard to provision.

In most cases, a stat-controlled halogen heat source fitted alongside a D3 linear or D3+ UVFLOOD is indeed required to provide the wild re-created index. Jungle Dawn LED plant-growth systems can be used alongside this lamp to increase further visible light, increase the CRI and, of course, cause live plants to flourish.

Of course, you can manipulate heat, light and lighting periods to cause the seasonal changes that are required for breeding. Certainly, with this group, if you are lucky enough to have your breeding plans coincide with a local drop in barometric pressure and a storm, it would be a great aid to the rain chamber!

Inverts and Bioactivity

I t would seem crazy to suggest that pet inverts should not be able to be kept in a Bio-Active fashion. They have, as we know, pretty much the exact same biological needs for both external and internal provision as every other life form, whereas they need regulated and controlled heat, food and water. In fact, most invert keepers have kept their pets in this method for many years already and have done so with quite spectacular results. Look at the sheer number and variety of Spiderlings that are available at any one time now. If only keepers were happy to only obtain a 2-3 cm spiderling and watch it grow instead of wanting larger, more impressive adults from day one, then there would now be very little need for wild captured animals to be imported at all.

Again, there is a method for every species. The arid species of scorpion, for example, could be kept on a good mix of organic earth and volcanic sands. Hardy springtails could be added to the lower levels of this substrate and then maintained. Live species of arid area grasses then could be propagated. This would act as a slice of the wild and should allow the animal to display natural behaviour. I myself keep a forest scorpion in a re-created forest

"A forest scorpion"

environment—and I assure you that this live-planted habitat is very much more enjoyable for me to view than the old style methods of keeping these incredible species in dark boxes. The scorpion also is very much more active and is very much more aggressive in both feeding and habitat maintenance than those that I have kept—and quite unsuccessfully so!—in the past.

"A captive bred Jungle Nymph"

Arboreal spiders could be kept in appealing tall live-planted vivaria. Again, the bio-culture can be maintained and LED or HOT5 plant-growth systems installed to allow sustained plant growth. We also are now starting to see the first glimpses of proven interaction with solar energy in inverts, with some D3 testing going on in 2014-15, which suggests a useful interaction. We have known, as I have written before, for some time, that certain species of spider seem to 'bask', or rather wave about, on the back legs for a few minutes when introduced to UVB and then disappear back off into the gloom, but we have never been able to prove the 'why'. This will change in time, and we will be given a definitive answer to this actually quite amusing puzzle.

Phasmids, of course, can benefit from the system but tend to very quickly eat the plants placed in their own home. As such, the propagation of these plants is very much more difficult. More thought needs to be put into these incredible and very enjoyable-to-keep species.

In all of this, we must remember that the theory of Wild Re-Creation™ through Bio-Activity is wholly reliant on the ability of a keeper being able to cater to inverts. As such, inverts take very well to the system, and should not pose too many problems at all.

In truth, we, as vertebrate keepers, have much to learn from our friends in the entomological side of the hobby. They have achieved much historically and continue to do so. However, I do feel that many of the species currently kept will be kept in larger and better designed terraria going forward, but that of course is the continued evolution of their own hobby.

"Giant African Millipede"

Odour Control

O ne of the age-old excuses that parents and loved ones have given for not allowing a pet reptile into the house is the fabled risk of smell. As experienced keepers ourselves, we all know that, on the whole reptiles, do not have a 'smell'. Yes, some species have foul odour excretions in times of stress, and every living thing has to pass its waste, but on the whole, reptiles are actually pretty clean and tidy. If the potential of odour release from an animal is indeed a real issue, then simply avoid those species that have this developed predator-avoidance mechanisms; musk turtles, garter snakes, dice snakes, milk snakes, indigo snakes, stinking goddesses and so on.

So, if reptiles do not smell, what is it that historically makes people think that they do? Well, the answer is very easy: poor care. Uncleaned and poorly maintained systems will putrefy and start to offend very quickly, especially those in which mammalian prey is offered. So, if we are purporting that Wild Re-Creation™ through Bio-Activity is the way forward, and that with this method there should be less need to actively clean, then what happens to the risk of smell?

A fully functioning Bio-Active system should never have a long-term offensive smell. They do have a musky almost woodland aroma to them, and that is the smell of health and wellbeing that we should use as a barometer to monitor the efficacy of our systems. Animal waste, of course, will continue to be laid, and it will have an odour, but in a fully functioning system we tend to see this waste and smell disappear very quickly indeed. This of course depends on the size and depth of the system and the potency/quantity of the custodians. It is highly unlikely, for instance, that a large Burmese python's waste matter could be dealt with in an hour inside of a system where the Bio-Active media was only a few inches deep. No, we have to use our brains and accept the realistic limitations to every aspect of the theory. Bigger animals will greatly benefit from Wild Re-Creation™ through Bio-Activity, but these systems will still require proactive regular maintenance and care. This, of course, is the opposite to a pair of day geckos living in a large Bio-Active system. The waste would be laid and not even be noticed by the keeper as the clean-up crew go to work and remove both waste and smell efficiently.

Live plants have a huge role to play here also. Yes, plants will utilise the animal's waste products as food, but they also will help to keep the air clean and fresh in their own right. I find that some of the species of fern work hard to remove waste and also reduce the risk of pooled water stagnation. Systems with an abundance of fibrous ferns seem to have an even clearer, fresher smell than those that do not. Essentially, the higher the level of planting, the easier the system will be to maintain in terms of smell and cleanliness, it will of course require more water, trimming and feeding.

A note on arboreal species: let us take the many day geckos as an example. As said, a pair of gold dust day geckos living in a healthy 60 x 45 x 90 Bio-Active system should never produce enough waste to cause a smell but, due to their habits, they will deposit such waste all over the plants, branches and glass. So, the custodians generally live in the soils, how can they possibly

"Standings Day Gecko"

clean up the waste that is left over the plants? In truth, they cannot. No, in the wild the rains and winds would arrive almost daily and the waste would be knocked or washed off of the plant and onto the floor where it would be consumed. It will have to be the same in captivity. A regular spray down will help, but as the keeper, you may need to step in and remove this waste entirely or simply knock it down into the substrate. Again, a level of proactive keeper interaction is always required. We therefore have a use and display interaction, but we also have a limitation. A compromise must be found.

Please do not give into the temptation to use propellant-based or wall socket-based room deodorisers. These can greatly affect both amphibian life and the reptilian respiratory system. I have heard of far too many collection meltdowns in rooms where these automated sprayers are used to be at all comfortable with their use. If you wish to scent a room, try a bowl of dried lavender and vanilla pods or other naturally fragrant dried flowers.

To conclude, with regard to the subject of odour control, if an odour problem becomes apparent, first look to a short falling in the system. Check the water level in the drainage layer and drain off or remove any access water manually (a large turkey baster can be used to push through the media and into the drainage

"Check the soil for water-logging and allow a sodden system to drain thoroughly and continue to remove any access until the soil has been fully drained."

layer, the water is then removed with the baster in systems without a physical drainage tap). Check the soil for water-logging and allow a sodden system to drain thoroughly and continue to remove any access until the soil has been fully drained. Add in more custodians. Tropical springtails will thrive in a wet system, meaning a couple of extra pots will help greatly as the system re-settles. Remove any unbroken down waste ASAP. Add in a worm manure-based soil food as this will help to provide essential nutrients to the custodians. Allow them to proliferate quickly and to get on with the job of re-starting the system. Watch for a day or so to see if the odour reduces: if it does, you are on the right road; carry as you are with careful maintenance and intervention where needed. If not, then further intervention and even a total system re-start may be required. However, this is very rare indeed.

Looking Forward as Forward Thinkers

The practice of continually looking forward is of course core to the fundamental goals of ethical and effective captive husbandry, regardless of the species that are to be kept. The same principles of care apply whether you keep snakes or frogs, degus or dogs. The core thinking behind the practise of learning from nature, from the actual biological processes and environmental interactions of a species and then implementing these in a safe and measured way, is simple and has to be constantly expanded upon over time.

There is no difference between the thought processes for the systems of care that are required for a vast breeding facility or zoological collection than there is for 'little Jonnie or Julie' who has a pet lizard, snake, frog or invertebrate. We can easily escalate up or down the daily tasks, products and processes that are required to affect Wild Re-Creation™ to suit the needs of any well-designed enclosure, and that is where the issues, problems and frustrations really lay.

As forward-thinking and ever-evolving keepers with constantly improving welfare at heart, we are only limited in the conversion of our thinking into reality by poorly thought out, poorly designed or hard to obtain products. Wild Re-Creation™ can never fulfil the core needs of a species if at first the enclosure is of the wrong shape or size or even both, nor if it has been so poorly thought out that even sustaining life within it would be a challenge to say the least. Glass tanks with poor ventilation and no safe heating or lighting method should be removed from stores, what possible use are they?

As ever-learning and forward-thinking keepers we actually have a huge say in the products that become available to the masses long-term. If we, as forward-thinking keepers, support those products that have a positive and effective use and then reversely refuse to buy those items that have come off of the pad of a designer rather than a designer who is also a keeper and understands the life support systems of exotics, then we will, in A very short shrift, see a positive move towards effective and ethical care in the hobby. The 'trash', whether that be substandard enclosures or poor electronics or potentially dangerous plastics, will have no consumer demand—and no demand means no manufacturer orders and that means that, as keepers, we are using our positive and educated thinking to affect a positive change and further adaption in the market. Practices and products will become better, prices will fall and, above all, the general level of welfare across the world will increase.

It is in the words 'forward-thinking' that we must remain constant and vigilant, never seemingly totally fulfilled with our systems and always seeking to further improve them to the benefit of our pets. As keepers, we should be happy with the quality and efficacy of our systems today but should also be keeping an eye and an ear on what may be required tomorrow. Forward-thinking does not stop when your own systems are set and functioning: there are always slight tweaks and adjustments that can be made and you may be surprised how effective a tiny adjustment can be

"Sheltopusik, Giant Glass Lizard"

in terms of increased levels of health and following on into long-term, sustainable and ethical reproduction.

We should also take into mind the constant improvements that are being made with regard to the accurate feeding of our pets. We still have so far to go on this subject that we may quite rightly surmise that we do indeed need a level of root and branch change. We should always be looking for and be willing to try any new species of live-food to feed to our pets when proven safe to do so. We should be forever researching and locating any pertinent new plants and any other organics for which a use could be found.

I think that we can all agree that a more rounded approach to the practice of full-spectrum feeding is all required but will, in all reality, take time. As such, our common goal of 'forward-thinking' can be the driving force that we all need to spur the hobby forward and to help to really make a difference both to captive pets and conservation collections alike. Remember: at home, keepers drive manufactures to find solutions and long-term answers.

In the last year, we have seen the retail inclusion of springtails and a number of other custodians become the norm alongside roaches, calciworms and, in terms of a new mammalian source, multimamates. If we could add another 6-12 new species or types of nutrition packed foods a year, we would very soon be able to not only supply for the core needs of any species but to cycle these diets in an effort to offer dietary variety and seasonality.

Therefore, we constantly look forward: we listen to each other and we come to an educated and well-balanced common understanding. This understanding must always have its foundations in the truth that 'today is better than yesterday but is nowhere near as good as tomorrow or the day after that or the day after that' and so on. We collectively and rigorously scrutinise new thinking to make sure that it has a place in the biological function and enrichment of a species and we weed out the dross in favour of allowing the positive to continually develop and to flourish.

This is modern-day reptile-keeping and it is very exciting indeed. Gone are the bad old days of a big python being kept in a box and bought out for a walk around the local town to scare the old people and here to stay are those stunning enclosures that really do provide for the core needs of any species that you may choose to incorporate into and to share your life with. Animals, after all, can and must never be thought of as commodities but rather as equals that deserve the very best that emerging science and technology can offer them.

A Word of Warning

I t is now quite clear to me that the well though-out provision of Wild Re-Creation™ through Bio-Activity is indeed a positive force and one that will propel captive husbandry into a new and ever-exciting dimension. The theory is indeed a 'mind set' and, as such, deserves—and, in reality, demands—a level of utter dedication. It is also very true to say that the nicest Bio-Active system, even when supplied with all of the 'bells and whistles' that science can afford, can go very wrong VERY quickly indeed, especially if the right level of maintenance is not afforded to it at all times.

Stagnation, unhelpful fungal and bacterial bloom and of course in reverse drying out can occur fairly rapidly and can cause a cataclysmic system meltdown. Both of these situations are likely to require an almost total restart of the entire system, which is to be avoided if at all possible. This forward-thinking theory represents a defined, driven and positive change within the hobby and the trade at a wider level. As such, we, as keepers, will need to accept that continued adaptation and careful implementation will always be required. In truth this is a level of captive care that has not, up until now, been required. As such, we are ALL still learning and we ALL will be always. A watchful, educated eye and the odd electronic device however can make this process very simple and indeed enjoyable. In truth, Bio-activity can become an all-encompassing obsession, especially when you see just how well your animals look and you see the positive results with regard to active and ethical reproduction—not to mention the ensuing obsession with live plant growth that will indeed and quite rapidly, take seed in your brain.

Obsession, in this case, is absolutely the right word. Wild Re-Creation™ through Bio-Activity can, for some of us, become all-encompassing and all-consuming. For those amongst us with an inquisitive mind, for those that love to spend time researching and developing ideas, this whole and updated, ever-evolving theory is a real godsend. It finally gives us something to get our teeth into and allows us then to share our knowledge far and wide. Wild Re-Creation™ through Bio-Activity is not a subject that should be held close to one's chest: no, every positive and negative experience must be shared willingly so that we can all learn from these global successes and failures and so that animal welfare remains paramount and ever-improving. It is, after all, the reason as to why we all invest such resource and time into the health and wellbeing of our pets.

"Malaysian Tree Toad"

I have, however, already seen and indeed been part of some very lively and fun online debates regarding the bulk of the theories behind the subject and again this type of interaction is on the whole a very positive thing. We can all learn through the written and the spoken word. By debating our own and other keeper's theories and observations we work to further expand our own and our collective knowledge base. This process is helpful and healthy, and ensures that there is always something new and exciting to mull over and to research, thus keeping the passion alive and active.

One point that was made on an online forum was with regard to just how far we should take the whole theory. If one was to truly enact Wild Re-Creation™, would that provision include replicating storms or droughts inside of our enclosures? Should we lower night time temperatures for desert species to 5 degrees or so? Should we starve our animals to re-create periods of lack and in the very extreme, what about stress, does the provision of stress and/or predator avoidance play an important part in the overall health and wellbeing of a species? After all, even caged bird breeders will use a single and separately caged cock song bird alongside their chosen breeding pairs to 'spur' the intended copulation forward by an act of almost jealousy. Is this Wild Re-Creation™ and does it have a place in our new world of positive care?

I can see where the writer of the question was coming from even if they were simply 'proving a point', all be it rather tongue in cheek. The theory of Wild Re-Creation™ through Bio-Activity has and must always have two fundamental and unbreakable principles. Principle A is that any inclusion into the system must be 'safe'. That, of course, means that good care is taken to protect both the animal and its keepers from all harm. The introduction of a predator to 'liven up' a captive pet therefore is and always will be ludicrous, as would be the critical lowering of an external temperature in a non-natural way. The principle of safety is paramount to the success of the system and to ever improving welfare. So yes, we Re-Create the parameters that a species has evolved to thrive under but we also afford them the luxury of not having to deal with a predator that is above them in the food chain in a confined space. There is, in captivity, of course, no chance of escape, and the level of stress and the knock-on effect to the animal's biology, including its mental health, will be far greater and far more detrimental than if it was simply running from a predator in the expanse of the wild. No, we view the protection of our chosen species as paramount and we avoid all potential causes of harm. We provide a safe and a secure home for life and view this provision just as essential as providing veterinary care if disease or injury was ever found.

"Asian Leaf Frog pair, a rare sight"

The second principle of Wild Re-Creation™ through Bio-Activity is thus: Principle B is everything that is added into or used in or around the subject animal must be measurable. We cannot measure any suggested positive impact that the risk of predation may have on the brain of a captive animal (if indeed there was any, which is extremely unlikely). We could very quickly see a whole host of negatives, however. As such, by simply following the principles of 'safe' and 'measured', we would very quickly come to realise that providing these many stresses and risks are neither safe nor measureable, and therefore must be avoided. The same can be said for food and decorative items, plastics, electricals, plants and, of course, any potential enclosure mates. If you cannot quantify it and be sure of success and safety, then you should omit introduction. (I have also seen many cases in my career of captive animals that have lived alone for long periods being reported as becoming either worryingly withdrawn or extremely aggressive when a new cage mate was introduced. As such you should seek to pair up those species that are social and will live in groups when the animals are younger rather than when they are old and before any territory has been designated. You should also ensure that you have a spare enclosure or have the ability to return any animal that may not be accepted into the enclosure. For many of us, a re-start of the enclosure is standard practise before introduction. Move around the decoration, swap the basking point around so that the old territory cannot be recognised. This sometimes works, but great care and a watchful eye will be required for quite some time after introduction with some species. Other species, such as the bearded dragon, of course should be kept alone as they maintain a wide territory in the wild and only seem to come together to breed and indeed fight. As such, for many enthusiasts, keeping more than one dragon in the same enclosure is a recipe for disaster. In fact, I have seen males become incredibly stressed and stop feeding just because they could see the reflection of another male in a separate vivarium below or above it. 'Outside of the box' thinking and planning therefore is always needed.)

What about night time heat? Okay, this is a basic principle of captive care for most, if not all, ectotherms. Yes, many reptiles and amphibians can tolerate wide temperate variances. Some can literally freeze by night and boil by day. Yes, the temperature in the desert can fall to almost freezing in parts of the world at night, and then rise to a blistering level of heat during the day. This does not mean that the animal would choose to expose themselves to these extreme levels of external energy in the home range. We must accept that the 'wild' is vastly different in terms of natural provision and evolution than a 4 x 2 x 2 wooden or glass box that is, by nature, stark and bare, with limited substrate or other hiding points. No, in reality, you will see in the wild that burrows and tunnels are used during these super-hot or colder times to great effect. These burrows, caves and tunnels offer very good protection from the extremities of the weather. They can also offer hydration, as we have already seen, but remember: they will store some heat from the sun during the day and then act like a blanket or shield all at once. The animal then can self-regulate its own core temperature by moving up or down the tunnel or even moving tunnels as it has need. This is a core survival technique that has worked for millennia. This is where our knowledge of the wild habitats of the species that we keep becomes very important. How many reports have you seen of wild bearded dragons sleeping out exposed in the scrublands all night long with no shelter or heat, not with a plastic cave over them while they sleep on cooling stone or even worse, on oil-based manmade tiles? No, the reports are that they have rock and tunnel networks that are used to find shelter and refuge. These are indeed used and they work well.

Compare this situation with your system at home. A night-time drop to 5 degrees may be tolerated for a while but, after a while, this will start to have a negative impact on the animal's body and brain alike. Why? Well, despite our best efforts, many of us do not have 3-4' deep substrates that allow effective tunnel-building.

We should use something like a stat-controlled ceramic heater or reptile radiator to provide a gentle night time heat without providing visible light."

Many still do not even use natural rock that will store and then radiate heat, nor do they use enough of it. As such, there are realistic limitations to the theory and there always will be. Again, go back to the checks and balances of 'safe' and 'measureable'. If your system is allowed to have a night time drop to 5 degrees in winter and you do not have this accurate level of wild mimicry in terms of the accurate provision of upper levels of daytime heat and the required replicated habitat your animal will not be able to find either shade from the blistering periods of the day nor protection from cold during the night. As such, we must be realistic and seek to provide a level of care that is proven to be safe and measureable.

In reality, we should use something like a stat-controlled ceramic heater or reptile radiator to provide a gentle night time heat without providing visible light. This will ensure that the animal does not have a lack of available energy below that of the wild animal and that a kind of permanent brumation is avoided. Many

"The accurate provision of controlled heat is vital for temperature sensitive species including pygmy chameleons"

feeding issues can simply be associated with the poor provision of or the under provision of heat.

We are all, I hope, active, keen and responsible keepers, or you simply would not be reading this book. As such, we should talk amongst ourselves, we should debate, and we should try new things willingly. Every keeper can learn from every other keeper and, on the whole, this passing on of knowledge is very positive indeed. However, we must remain dedicated to welfare and propagation. As such, the extremes of Wild Re-Creation™, as in the provision of predation stress and artificially low or high solar/thermal gradients, must be removed at all costs.

It will, in time, be possible to re-create both lighting, rain and wind inside of those systems that could tolerate and benefit from such a thing. This could be useful in terms of aiding gaseous exchange and, of course, with the provision of periods of high humidity and hydration. It may even play a positive role in breeding cycles and mental wellbeing if maintained correctly. (It is already very common to use rain chambers with many species of captive amphibian to spur on breeding and the laying of spawn.) I have no issue with this when safe to do so and when technology allows. What we cannot do is replicate the changes in barometric pressure that come with wild storms; in reality, we would only be replicating part of the total experience for them. Again, time will tell, and it will be, if nothing else, quite exciting.

I would also take this opportunity to write briefly about the accurate waterproofing of the many electricals that are now used within our varying systems. Vivariums and terrariums, on the whole, are very hot and humid environments; some having mist and spray/rain systems; some are actually quite wet. As such, there is a standard with regard to electricals that should be observed to maintain high levels of safety for both animal and keeper. This is now law in the EU with regard to aquariums.

Please ensure that all electricals placed inside of a wet system carry the formal IP67 rating. The IP67 standard will ensure that the electrical fitting is indeed waterproof. IP68 is referred to as being submersible and IP64 as being splash proof, and is most suited to the more arid system where direct spraying is less likely to occur.

It is also very difficult indeed to waterproof any fitting that has a bayonet or E26/E27 screw thread. As such, these fittings must, for safety's sake, be placed outside of the wet/humid areas and away from direct water ingression. In the case of Arcadia Jungle Dawn, for example, and being LED, it can be placed quite successfully above a mesh or even glass without a great reduction in light levels or of course PAR.

Heat lamps also must be placed away from direct sources of water. Cold water splashing onto superheated glass will likely cause explosion. I have recently started to use the ReptiRadiator in our systems. This product also offers a greater level of protection from water.

Drip loops also can be used to further ensure electrical integrity. Please follow the instructions that are sure to be found inside if the box of any new equipment that you add into your system.

Timers, of course, are a welcome addition into many systems, but the old adage of you get what you pay for is certainly true here.

"A fringe Toe Lizard"

Many of the cheaper mechanical timers can allow a power surge as the product turns an electrical item on and off. Paying that little bit extra should ensure a good electrical supply and go some way to both protecting and lengthening the life of the electrical item that you wish to control. Many timers are also now fitted with an electrical surge protector. Again, this is a clever piece of electronics that will help to filter out power variances and once again can help to protect and prolong the life of an electrical item. It is indeed surprising just how many electricals are 'killed off' with surges in the local power supply.

What is Right for One may not be Right for All

or me, the theory of Wild Re-Creation™ though Bio-Activity, applied in a safe and measured way, is by far the most positive change to captive husbandry in many years. Okay, it is my theory, I am slightly biased, but I must point out that, even if the theory appears to be as sound on paper as it does in practise in my own experiments, it cannot be thought of as safe for every keeper on the planet all of the time and in every situation. For a start, as I have said previously, there are animals in our collections that are either unsuited to or have medical complaints that negate the use of the Bio-Active system.

In a similar way, there are many good keepers out there that either do not have the time nor the inclination to bring these methods en-masse into a large collection and of course there are new or younger keepers for which the time is simply not right—yet. As always, animal welfare must always come first. If there is any chance at all that an animal may suffer either due to poor health or from a poor understanding and implementation of the theory by the keeper, then the theory should be avoided until such a time when either the animal is in a stable enough condition to be able to benefit from a more wild-like existence or when the keeper has gained enough knowledge and experience to be able to implement the theory in this safe and measured way. As such, there should never be any propensity to guilt. We, as keepers, are all 'family', dedicated to this natural 'underworld', helping each other and not hindering. A Bio-Active keeper should never put pressure upon a sterile keeper that is not entirely comfortable with the theory or is not ready to implement. Welfare is paramount. I would rather see a fit and healthy animal living on natural slates than one that is not cared for properly, living in what was 'once' and full of good intentions, a Bio-Active system.

This is the start of something new. As always, 'new' can be a scary place and a place that is forever changing and adapting. The theory is not right for everyone just yet, but I sincerely believe that, as the years progress and as we all continue to learn, we will, on the whole, move into this theory of Wild Re-Creation™ through Bio-Activity.

Conclusion

A s I set out to write down this guide, I had a clear idea of what I thought I may go on to discover in terms of the wild habitats and increasing the levels of captive welfare and reproduction. I had assumed that I would see a link between Bio-Activity, feeding and health, and that I would be able to shout about how basic it all was. In truth, nothing could possibly have prepared me for the almost Pandora's Box of possibilities that my research and practical experiments exposed, and then repeatedly opened up over the eighteen months of research that I conducted and continue to do so. The clear link between the world's wild environments and its inhabitants at every level was not a subject that I thought would be both so complex and so easy to replicate, not to mention such a joy to discover.

As so-called 'forward-thinking keepers', I believe that we are now on the cusp of something truly wonderful. A new age of taking basic scientific thought and paperbound theories and then proving or disproving them in the real world with the common goal of improving animal welfare at every level. As always, thoughts and practises change and adapt and, on the whole, should get

"Azureus blue dart frog"

better and better as time progresses. It therefore is up to us, as individual keepers, to continue to change and to adapt, yes to evolve, and to forcibly propel this evolution forward through both active research in the home and by supporting those others that seek to make the life of captive exotics better.

For me, it was the realisation that the micro world of earth-bound vitamins, minerals and, of course, the vast culture of live entities that it houses and that has an active and real impact on the health and wellbeing of every other part of that eco-system that was so very useful. This is without doubt a true

"Monitor lizards benefit greatly from having space to dig and to find food."

and potent continuous 'symbiosis' of life. Every species, every element, and every external force working alongside and with each other to sustain each other, whether that is by paying the ultimate price and ending up as food or as something as simple as calcium being so abundant in the world's soils and waters, and helping to allow the correct levels of biological function over every other part of the chain. Yes, in my mind, there is a world of discovery to still make use of. The pathway towards Bio-Activity and Wild Re-Creation™ in captive collections is indeed a positive force but we must never assume that it the whole answer.

Bio-Activity is not and should never be thought of as simply the growing of live plants inside of an enclosure. It is not even the further addition of springtails into the media. Both of these elements of care are part of Bio-Activity and Wild Re-Creation™, but the use of just these two elements do not make for a truly Bio-Active system. No, Bio-Activity and Wild Re-Creation™ is all encompassing, it is all-consuming and works from the micro level upwards. As such, we must start to think of our enclosures themselves as 'life support' systems rather than as a simple box in which an animal can call home. Yes, it is more than possible to keep a reptile in a sterile glass or wooden tank on aspen or orchid bark or tiles or newspaper, but how can that possibly be providing all that it needs as per the historical evolution of the species. If a species has a need to ingest parts of its eco-system, then that is part of its core evolution and should not only be a safe but an active and potent force of supply in and of itself.

The earth is a provider! She is not just there to grow plants and to give us as humans something to stand upon—no, it is within this 'earth' that we will find many of the secrets of great captive care. The earth or soil is a life force teaming with minerals and vitamins, especially those critical members of the B group. It acts as source of calcium, potassium, sulphur, silicon, magnesium, iron, manganese, cobalt, zinc, copper and many, many more. Earth/soil contains organic plant and animal matter, faeces and, of course, core life itself from the invert that dwell within it, both great and micro right the way down to the amoebic. Each and every part works together, largely in balance, to sustain our planet and everything residing on and within it. If we can truly realise the importance of this 'life' as an entity and then start to work to re-create that in a safe and measured way, we will, as a group, have broken the back of new discovery and will have opened a gateway into a world of almost miraculous new discovery.

As my research continued, I started to see more and more the essential uses of water and the many ways that water acts as the glue that holds all life together. I had already written in my previous works about water and its correct 'species' provision, but I must admit that further research started to show more and more ever-strengthening links between the correct provision of water and the symbiosis of all of the elements that we call life. Yes, simply spraying down a viv in a pertinent manner is a positive thing for those transfer drinkers, but we must not overlook ground born humidity and the miracles of drinking by capillary action. This then led on to rethinking the correct provision, filtration and circulation of water, and how to stop a build-up of humidity becoming a negative force. One aspect of

"Acanthasaura lepidogaster showing good colour"

care that we lack in captive enclosures is wind and drainage. As such, we have had to take these limitations and find an answer. It was clear to me that, even in the answer, whether that be the addition of fans or drainage layers and drainage taps or thirsty plants, that there were further indications to positive care.

We therefore must see an ecosystem as a living, breathing entity. If we change our perspective to keeping habitats rather than just the animals themselves, we then can, by definition, keep and breed the animals of our desire in an ethical and effective way.

This, my friends, is the very life behind the idea, the concept, the force, the ever-changing and improving process we refer to as 'Wild Re-Creation™ through Bio-Activity'

Thanks

Writing a book is a laborious process fraught with delays and daily stresses, and believe me I suffered with both of these whilst compiling this series. As always, I must thank my wife, Sue, and my son, Aaron, for their continued support and encouragement, without such I could simply never even consider the task. Thanks go to my parents for introducing me to, and nurturing within me a love for, nature and the wonderful world of exotic animal care. Thanks to the directors of Arcadia Reptile who have shown such trust and ongoing support.

There are a few individuals that I wish to thank personally. For me, 'learning' is a very verbal process. As such, I speak to as many professionals and at-home keepers as possible, and use this collective cache of knowledge to come up with my basic thoughts and theories. As such, I thank the following—you really do not know how much I value our 'chats': Peter Blake (big yellow gecko), Steve day, Dave Laux, Pete Morris, Adam singleton, Adam Hough, Mark Amey, Siouxsie Gillett, Dr Mike Leahy, Todd Goode, Tim Green, Dave Perry, Stuart Worth, Peter Foulsham, Jo Wise, Sue Patterson, Jason Miller, Rhianna Sly, Luke Harding, Iri Gill, Geoff

Clarke, James Hardie, Calvin Allen, Ron Eddy, Paul Wiley, Francis Cosquieri, Shaun Dixon, Shaun Madder, Ben Tapley, Andrew Grey, Adam Bland and Tarron Boon.

As always, there are two people that deserve my ongoing and special thanks: David Alderton and Frances Baines. Both have demonstrated a lifetime's dedication to improving pet welfare and sincerely deserves a medal!

I also wish to point out how useful I have found the educational resources and weekly updates from the Royal Society of Biology. To have been made a member is something I consider a great honour.

Glossary of terms

Alfalfa: Alfalfa or Lucerne is a widely grown crop plant that has a high Ca content and appears to attract insect life to itself. It is a very balanced food source and should certainly be viewed to replace bran as an insect and reptile food. Alfalfa has been grown and used for thousands of years and has many nutritional and medicinal properties.

Arboreal: This is the word used to describe animals that spend much of their life in the trees and shrubs.

Bee Pollen: Bee pollen is obtained from harvesting pollen gathered by worker bees from male flowers. Millions of grains of pollen are required to manufacture one small grain. Bee pollen may be useful in reptile care as an additive to gut loading formulas and as a supplementary food source.

Bio-Active: A blanket term used to describe a method of keeping an enclosure as being truly 'live'. Bio-Active refers to the functioning symbiosis of all of the separate elements of the system from the provision of a live substrate and pertinent plants through to the interaction of the animal with its enclosure. This will help to ensure that the target animal species can benefit from this more natural surrounding and display natural behaviour. Bio-Activity is a cyclical method in which animal waste and plant matter are converted by the custodians into readily available and biologically useful foods and elements.

Brumation: A brumation is the term used to describe the autumn/winter slowdown of an animal. In this time they will become less active, eat and bask less, and spend much more time sleeping. Brumation is not a full hibernation, and times of activity will be visible. A brumating animal should not lose weight. If any animal enters a sudden or long brumation, veterinary advice should be sought immediately.

Ca: This is the chemical symbol for Calcium. This is the mineral responsible for building and maintaining healthy bones, muscle contraction and maintaining a healthy blood supply.

Calciworm: Calciworm is the British name for the larva of the black soldier fly. In the US, it is also known as the Phoenix Worm. This is becoming a live food of choice gradually owing to its lower fat but good Ca-P ratio.

Crepuscular: This is the term used to describe animals that are more commonly seen as being active at dawn and dusk. This behaviour may be because of the animal's evolved sensitivity to light or as a long-term predator-avoidance measure. Crepuscular animals tend to have a very thin skin and slit shaped contracting pupils.

Constipation: This is the term used to describe an animal's inability to pass waste in an easy and effective manner. Constipation is usually caused by a lack of fibre and dehydration and should not be confused with 'impaction'.

Custodian: The blanket term used to describe the many species of usually invertebrate that can be introduced into a Bio-Active system. All of which perform a useful task in terms of enclosure maintenance and nutrition to both plants and animals alike

D3 cycle: The ability to produce and use Vitamin D3 inside of an animal's body after exposure to natural sunlight.

Diurnal: This is the word used to describe an animal that is primarily more active during the day.

Endo-thermic: The term used to describe an animal that obtains the energy that is required directly from digested food rather than from the sun alone (warm blooded).

Ecto-thermic: The term used to describe an animal that obtains its energy directly from heat from the sun rather than from food, (cold blooded).

Enrichment: Enrichment is a term used to describe useful, provided for behavioural stimulation inside of an enclosure or indeed in the wild. Historically we have only really thought of enrichment being associated with enclosure decoration, places to hide, places to hunt etc. In reality enrichment should cover every sector of the provision for a species. Enclosure size and decoration, water provision, finding food and self-supplementation, heat and light can all be thought of as stimulators and as such can play a positive role in enrichment.

Faecal Screening: A small sample of the animal's waste matter that is sent to a lab to access any bacterial or parasitical load, diagnosis can then be given and treatment advised if required. This is a fairly common procedure that can be undertaken through the post.

Foliar misting/feeding: To spray or to mist the leaves of a plant with either water or water with a suitable, organic, reptile and amphibian safe food source.

Full-spectrum: Full-spectrum is a term used to describe a total inclusion of a 'factor'. In terms of light we refer to 'full-spectrum' as being all of the terrestrial wavelengths catered for in a safe and balanced way. In terms of nutrition this refers to the provision of every nutrition requirement being catered for just as it would in the wild without exception.

Gut-loading: This is the term used to describe the practice of accurately feeding and hydrating insects that are to be used as live food before they are in turn fed to an animal.

Hydrometer: A small mechanical or now digital device that can also be incorporated into some digital thermometers and used to measure the level of moisture inside of an enclosure.

Hypervitaminosis: This is the term used to describe an oversupply of a certain vitamin.

Hypovitaminosis: This is the term used to describe an undersupply of a certain vitamin.

I.R: I.R is the abbreviated term for 'Infra-Red. Infra-red is invisible radiant energy at the far end of the light spectrum past visible red. With regard to reptile care we use this to refer to heat.

Impaction: This is the term used to describe a build-up of foreign bodies inside of the stomach and intestines of an animal. Common causes of impaction are ingested sands and artificial media. If left untreated, impaction is often fatal.

LED: stands for 'light emitting diode'. A low energy source of light that is usually quite specific in terms of wavelength and requires a low provision of energy to produce a large volume of light. In this case and at this time it is not possible to find a commercial LED that provides both visible light and UV. Those that do, only project a very narrow range of wavelengths to a pitiful and as such unhelpful distance.

MBD (Metabolic Bone Disorder/Disease): This as is commonly known is a condition that affects captive animals via a depletion of stored calcium and phosphorous reserves from the bones. In reality MBD can be used as a blanket term for any of the nutritional deficiencies.

Minerals: Oxford University describes the definition of a mineral as, 'A mineral is a naturally occurring inorganic solid, with a definite chemical composition, and an ordered atomic arrangement. This may seem a bit of a mouthful, but if you break it down it becomes simpler'.

Nocturnal: The term used to describe those animals that are only typically found being active at night.

PAR: The abbreviated term used to describe 'Photosynthetic Active Radiation'. This is the amount of energy that is available from light, typically when referred to when discussing levels of plant growth.

Parasite: A parasite is a secondary organism that lives inside of or upon the body of a host animal. They obtain nutrients directly from the host and can infect the vital organs in some cases. Regular screening is a sensible husbandry practise.

P: Phosphorous is an essential element to life. It works alongside many other vitamins and minerals, including Ca and Vitamin B and Vitamin D, so as to allow essential nutrient assimilation and use inside of the body.

Photogradient: The term used to describe a gradient of bright light being graduated into equal shade.

Photoperiod: This is the term used to describe the amount of hours a day that light source is provided throughout an enclosure.

Slate: An easy to find natural stone that can be stuck or dowel joined together to make rock networks. Natural slate is a very dense rock and as such will both reflect and store heat. The use of natural slate can be viewed as essential to the accurate maintenance of the theory.

SolarMeter: SolarMeter is actually a brand name for a handheld device that is used to measure wavelengths of light. In terms of usability in the hobby we suggest that the SolarMeter 6.5 Index metre is used.

Solar Recreation: Recreating the average level of solar exposure of a species in captivity as it would expect to find and to use in the wild.

Supplements: Describing natural and/or synthetic vitamin and mineral powders that can be added to an animal's diet to supplement dietary shortfalls of important elements.

Tetrachromacy: This is the addition of a fourth cone cell in the eye of birds, reptiles and some fish. This cell allows these species with the addition of UVA to see a vast array of otherwise invisible colours.

The Light and Shade Method: This is the practice of providing a UVB-rich light source over a targeted area that mimics the upper safe UVindex as experienced by a species in the wild. This is then matched with good access to cool and shade at the opposite end of the enclosure so as to allow the animal to self-regulate its own level of exposure at will.

Thermogradient: This is the term used to describe a gradient of temperatures from hot at one side of an enclosure to cool at the other in which a species can choose its own level of power (energy). This is usually matched with the provision of light.

Thermometer: A mechanical or digital device used to measure temperature.

Thermostat: An electrical device, either mechanical or digital that allows a keeper to dictate and to regulate the temperature to which a heat source maintains an environment.

UVA: Ultra Violet A , the wavelengths of light in the violet end of the spectrum as described between 320 nm and 400 nm.

UVB: Ultra Violet B, the wavelengths of light in the violet end of the spectrum as described between 280 nm and 320 nm.

UVC: Ultra Violet C, a non-terrestrial wavelength of light. It is highly dangerous as it destroys life at the cellular level. Any UVC is blocked by the earth's atmosphere.

UVI: UVI is the abbreviated term for 'UV Index'. The UV index is an international measurement used to quantify the strength of terrestrial levels of UV. It is commonly used by meteorologists to show the power of the sun and the associated risk of dermal burn to humans as part of a forecast. As such this measurement can be used quite accurately to recreate local habitat quantities of ultraviolet inside of the modern vivarium and terrarium. This quantity can therefore be relied upon to affect Wild Re-Creation™. Remember however that just because a habitat shows a very high index, it does not mean that your pet would choose to expose itself to that index or quantity of power at its apex nor would it be safe. No, most reptiles would find shade in the hottest, strongest periods of the day or only allow parts of the body to be exposed through rock or leaf scatter patterns. This is self-regulation and is the reason why the light and shade method is so vastly important.

Viv: Vivarium/Terrarium, recognised as an enclosure in which a reptile, invertebrate or amphibian can live.

Vitamin: As per the Oxford English Dictionary, 'Any of a group of organic compounds which are essential for normal growth and nutrition and are required in small quantities in the diet because they cannot be synthesized by the body: *most people can get all the vitamins they need from a healthy diet'.*

Volcanic rock: Volcanic rock is an organic and naturally mined gravel or sand taken from volcanic activity. It is wholly natural and contains a broad spectrum of very useful natural minerals.

Wild Re-Creation™: The theory of Wild Re-Creation™ aims to provide a truly holistic approach to the husbandry of any and all given species. It relies upon the idea that every species has changed and developed in a myriad of ways over a vast period of time to truly thrive in its own ecosystems in the wild. If we as keepers mimic those parameters then we will by definition be supplying everything that any given species needs to thrive also in captivity.

Worm Manure: The nutrient rich excretions from the earthworm. These are also referred to as 'castings'. They are largely from a certified organic source and can play an important role with regard to feeding a system

VOC: The abbreviated term for 'Volatile organic compound'. Typically refers to the leeching or release of toxins from one source after an interaction with another, i.e. plastics or resins when heated to a certain temperature.

X-ray: As with humans, reptiles and amphibians can easily be X-rayed at most veterinary practices. An X-ray will help the vet to access bone density and could show up other underlying diseases and of course the rate of bone repair.